Michael Price

Windows 8.1 for Seniors

Also covers Windows RT 8.1

In easy steps is an imprint of In Easy Steps Limited
16 Hamilton Terrace · Holly Walk · Leamington Spa
Warwickshire · United Kingdom · CV32 4LY
www.ineasysteps.com

Notice of Liability
Every effort has been made to ensure that this book
contains accurate and current information. However, In
Easy Steps Limited and the author shall not be liable for
any loss or damage suffered by readers as a result of
any information contained herein.

Trademarks
Microsoft® and Windows® are registered trademarks
of Microsoft Corporation. All other trademarks
are acknowledged as belonging to their respective
companies.

In Easy Steps Limited supports The Forest Stewardship
Council (FSC), the leading international forest
certification organisation. All our titles that are printed
on Greenpeace approved FSC certified paper carry the
FSC logo.

MIX
Paper from
responsible sources
FSC® C020837

Printed and bound in the United Kingdom

ISBN 978-1-84078-615-6

Contents

12 Networking   207

13 Security & Maintenance   219

Index   233

1 Get Windows 8.1

This chapter explains how Windows 8.1 has evolved from previous releases, identifies the new features and helps you recognize what's needed to upgrade your existing computer. Your Microsoft account makes your settings portable. You can choose to sign in to the Start screen or Desktop, and you can install Windows apps.

Windows 8.1

Windows 8.1 is the latest release of Microsoft Windows, the operating system for personal computers. There has been a long list of Windows releases including:

- 1995   Windows 95
- 1998   Windows 98
- 2000   Windows Me (Millennium Edition)
- 2001   Windows XP (eXPerience)
- 2003   Windows XP MCE   (Media Center Edition)
- 2007   Windows Vista
- 2009   Windows 7
- 2012   Windows 8 (and Windows RT)
- 2013   Windows 8.1 (and Windows RT)

When you buy a new computer, it is usually shipped with the latest available release of Windows. This takes advantage of the hardware features generally available at the time. Every year sees new and more powerful features being incorporated into the latest computers. In line with this, the requirements for Microsoft Windows have increased steadily. For example, the minimum and recommended amounts of system memory have increased from Windows 95 (4MB to 8MB), Windows 98 (16MB to 24MB), Windows XP (64MB to 128MB), Windows Vista (512MB to 1024MB), Windows 7 and Windows 8/8.1 (1GB to 2GB). There's a similar progression in terms of the processor power, the video graphics facilities and hard disk storage.

This means that your computer is likely to need upgrading or extending in order to use a later release of Windows, especially if you want to take advantage of new capabilities such as multi-touch. To take full advantage of new features, you may need a new computer, for example a "tablet" PC.

Each release enhances existing features and adds new facilities. Thus, the new Windows 8.1 is able to support all the functions of Windows 8, Windows 7 and prior releases, often with enhancements, plus its own unique new features.

This allows you to use your computer to carry out tasks that would not have been possible with previous system releases.

Don't forget

There have been other releases of Microsoft Windows, intended for business and server computers, including Windows NT, Windows 2000, Windows Server 2003, Windows Server 2008 and Windows Server 2012.

Hot tip

Windows RT is the version of Windows 8 and 8.1 that is designed for tablet PCs that use the ARM processor, as used in cell phones and other hand-held devices.

Hot tip

Windows 8.1 is an in-service update to Windows 8 that provides features and functions to make it easier to switch from previous systems.

Which Release is Installed?

To check which release of Windows is currently installed on your system, you can look in System properties.

1 Press WinKey + Break key or right click the Start button and click System to display the Properties

2 The operating system details will be displayed (along with user, memory and processor information)

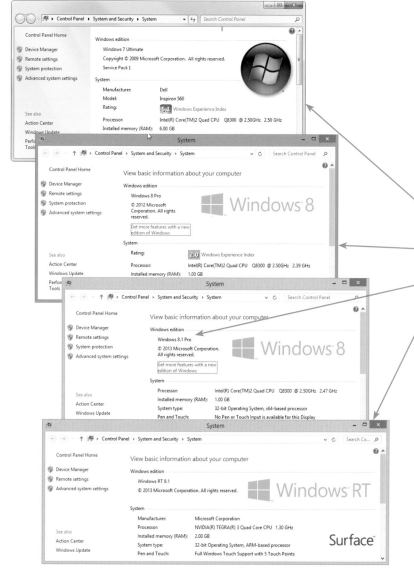

Don't forget

WinKey is normally used to represent the Windows Logo key. Break key is the one normally labeled Pause/Break.

Don't forget

These images show the System properties for computers with:

Windows 7

Windows 8

Windows 8.1

Windows RT 8.1

Hot tip

This shows Windows edition and service level, plus other details that may vary between releases. For example, Windows 8.1 does not display Experience Index (system rating).

11

Hot tip

The Start screen replaces the Start menu of previous releases of Windows. The Desktop is used for traditional Windows applications.

Don't forget

There are some new Windows 8.1 apps and some traditional desktop applications provided with Windows 8.1 at installation, but you will need to visit the Windows Store for many functions that were previously included.

Features of Windows 8.1

Tile-based User Interface

Windows 8.1 features a tile-based user interface, similar to the interface for the Windows Phone and optimized for touchscreens as well as mice and keyboards. The Start screen displays live application tiles which start Windows 8.1 apps. These run full-screen, or two can be displayed side-by-side on higher resolution (1366 × 768 and larger) monitors.

Windows 8.1 also displays a login/lock screen that shows the date and time and notifications, along with a customizable background.

Windows Store

Windows Store is a digital distribution application that is the only means of distributing Windows 8.1 apps to users. Microsoft will scan apps for security flaws and malware. Apps may be free or may carry a charge for download.

The Windows Store also allows developers to publish traditional desktop applications, providing links to those applications on the developer websites.

File Explorer

Access to files, folders and drives is provided by the new version of Windows Explorer, now known as File Explorer, which now includes a Ribbon interface to provide in-context access to commands.

Restore and Reset

With Windows 8.1 you can refresh your PC, which keeps all your documents, accounts, personal settings and modern apps but returns Windows to its original state. You can completely restore your PC to the state it was in when you first got it.

You can create a recovery drive on a USB key with the files needed to refresh or reset your PC even if Windows 8.1 can't boot. Restoring from the USB drive is a good option if you have a tablet PC without a disc drive or you just want to save space.

Shorter Start-up Times

Windows 8.1 has short boot times, because it saves the kernel's memory to the hard disk on shutdown (similar to the existing hibernate option) and reloads it on start up.

Internet Explorer 11

The latest version of the Windows web browser, Internet Explorer 11, dedicates the entire screen to your websites, giving a full edge-to-edge display. Only when you need them do the browser tabs and navigation controls appear and they quietly get out of the way when you don't want them anymore. By taking advantage of Windows 8.1 and your computer's hardware acceleration features, Internet Explorer makes browsing faster and more fluid and the security capabilities ensure that your access is safe.

Microsoft Account Integration

Your Windows User account is linked to your Microsoft account. This means that you will not lose your settings and files as you move from your home computer to your work laptop, or to any other computer also using Windows 8.1 and sign in via your Microsoft account.

Multiple Monitors

If you have multiple monitors, Windows 8.1 can span the taskbar across the desktop on each of the monitors. Similarly, you can show different wallpapers on different monitors, or the same wallpaper stretched across multiple monitors.

Removed Features

Several features that were present in Windows 7 and prior releases are no longer available in Windows 8. The Start menu and the Start button were removed, although a form of Start button has been restored to Windows 8.1. The Aero Glass themes have been replaced by Windows 8 themes. The Microsoft Gadgets Gallery has also been removed. Windows Media Center is not included and Windows Media Player does not provide DVD playback.

Some features are only available in particular editions of Windows 8.1, or have specific hardware prerequisites.

13

The Windows Media Center will be available for purchase as an add-on and this will include DVD playback capability.

The terms 32-bit and 64-bit relate to the way the processor handles memory. You'll also see the terms x86 and x64 used for 32-bit and 64-bit respectively.

Beware

The product functions and the graphics capabilities may vary depending on the system configuration.

What's Needed

The minimum configuration recommended by Microsoft to install and run Windows 8.1 is as follows:

- Processor   1GHz 32-bit or 64-bit

- System memory   1GB (32-bit) or 2GB (64-bit)

- Graphics   DirectX 9 graphics device with WDDM 1.0 driver

- Hard disk drive   16GB (32-bit) or 20GB (64-bit) free

- Optical drive   DVD/CD (for installation purposes)

There may be additional requirements for some features, for example:

- SVGA display monitor with 1024 x 768 or higher resolution (1600 × 1200 to snap three Windows apps)

- Internet access for online services and features such as Windows Update

- TV tuner for Windows Media Center functions

- Five point Multi-touch hardware for touch functions

- A network and multiple PCs running Windows 8.1 for HomeGroup file and printer sharing

- An optical drive with rewriter function for DVD/CD authoring and backup function

- Trusted Platform Module (TPM) 1.2 hardware for BitLocker encryption

- USB flash drive for Windows to Go/BitLocker To Go

- An additional 1GB memory, 15GB extra hard disk space and a processor with Intel VT or AMD-V hardware features, for Hyper-V virtualization

- Audio output (headphones or speakers) for music and sound in Windows Media Player

...cont'd

4 To display the desktop, click the Desktop tile on the Start screen, or the Desktop App entry on the Apps screen

Hot tip

Windows Accessories and conventional Windows applications, designed for previous versions of Windows, are run in the Desktop environment.

5 The Desktop will be displayed

6 Note the Start button and the application icons on the Taskbar

7 Desktop for Windows RT 8.1 is similar but features icons on the Taskbar for Office 2013 applications

Don't forget

Windows RT 8.1 has a special version of Office 2013, and includes associated tiles on the Start screen, as well as icons on the Taskbar.

8 Click the Start button on the Taskbar to return to the Start screen or press WinKey (the Windows Logo key)

23

Windows 8.1 Update

If you have a PC that is still running Windows 8, Windows Store will also provide the update for the system:

1 Visit the Windows Store and you will be offered the option to Update to Windows 8.1 for free

2 Click the panel to see more details of the update

3 Click Download and follow the prompts

Don't forget

If your PC is currently running Windows 8 or Windows RT, it's free to update to Windows 8.1 or Windows RT 8.1. And you'll get this update from the Windows Store.

Hot tip

The process updates or replaces some of your existing built-in apps. Other existing Windows Store apps don't transfer, but once the update is complete, you can reinstall as many as you need (see page 132 for Your apps).

Install Windows Apps

There are many Windows apps in the Windows Store, but Microsoft spotlights sets of apps that can make good starting points. To review and install these:

1 From the Start screen, click Store, which opens as a full screen Windows app

2 You see a changing display of highlighted apps plus a group of apps picked for you

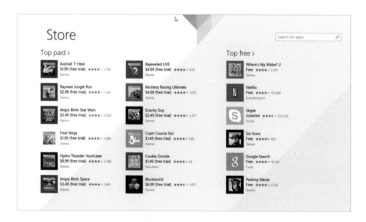

3 Scroll right to see groups of Trending apps, New & Rising, Top Paid and Top Free apps

Don't forget

Applications designed for the Windows 8.1 environment can be downloaded and installed from the Windows Store, a procedure familiar to users of smartphones and tablet devices.

Hot tip

The apps shown take into account the type of operating system, e.g. Windows 8.1 or Windows RT 8.1, and also the type of system, e.g. specific entries appear for a Microsoft Surface.

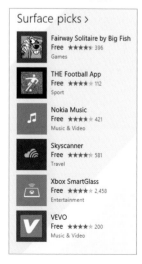

...cont'd

Hot tip

When you Install an app, the Store reappears and you see progress messages at the top right of the screen. You can select another app, even if previous installs are still pending.

Don't forget

Entries for the apps that you install are added to the Apps screen into the appropriate area, and positioned alphabetically by name.

4 Select an app, e.g. Cocktail Flow, to see the description

5 Click the Install button if you want to add the app, then review and install any other apps you want

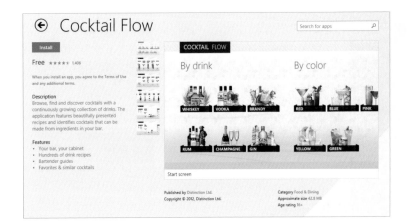

6 Go to the Apps screen to see the additions (Tiles are not automatically added to the Start screen though you can add them yourself (see page 69)

2 Windows 8.1 Interface

Windows 8.1 uses the tile-based interface first seen in Windows 8. It is designed for touch operation, while still supporting keyboard and mouse. It features Hotspots and Charms and new ways to start up apps and to close them down.

The start-up time depends on the configuration of your computer and on how it was previously closed, but usually it is less than a minute.

This is the default Lock screen image, but you can choose another image from the Picture library, or even play a slide show on the Lock screen.

Start Windows 8.1

Switch on your computer to start up the operating system. The stages are as follows:

1 A simple Windows logo is displayed, with a rotating cursor to show that the system is being loaded

2 After a while, the Lock screen is displayed

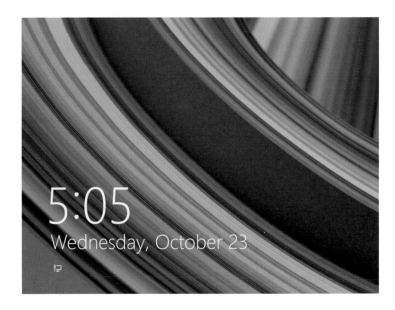

3 Press a key or click a mouse button, or sweep up on a Touch monitor, to display the user Logon screen

4 Type the password and click the arrow (or press the Enter key)

5 The Welcome message is displayed while the user account settings are being applied

6 The Windows 8.1 Start screen is displayed, showing the tile-based Windows 8.1 apps currently available

Don't forget

If there are multiple user accounts, you may need to select the required account before signing on (see page 30).

Hot tip

The use of a Microsoft account, as indicated by the display of an email address, means you can download and install apps from the Windows Store.

Don't forget

If you have changed the Navigation settings (see page 136) you could start up with the Desktop or the Apps screen displayed.

Multiple User Accounts

Don't forget

If there is more than one user account, the Logon screen will display the last used account, with a Back Arrow button to show all the accounts.

1 Click the Back Arrow button, and then click the user account that you wish to sign in with

2 Enter the password to sign in to the selected account

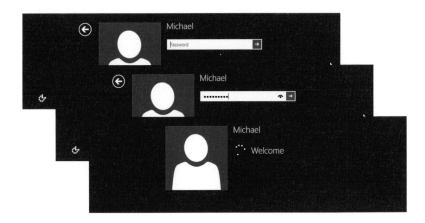

Hot tip

Since there's no email address shown for the selected user account in this example, you know the account is Local rather than Microsoft, and so cannot be used to download from the Microsoft Store.

3 The Start screen (or alternative initial screen for that account) will be displayed

Start Screen Layout

The appearance of the Start screen is much more akin to the smartphone, for example the Windows Phone, rather than the startup screens of previous versions of Windows. There's no Start button or Taskbar, though these do appear on the Desktop. There are groups of tiles that invoke Windows apps, so the Start screen acts as a substitute for the Start menu. The actual contents of the Start screen depend on what customization and enhancements you (or your PC supplier) have applied. However, you can expect to find:

Towards the top right of the Start screen is the username and picture (which can be personalized – see page 66).

Windows Apps   Live Tiles   App Group   Username and Picture

Desktop App   Display Apps screen   Scroll Bar   Zoom Button

Some of the important features of the Start screen and the Desktop – Hotspots and the Charms bar – are actually out of sight (see page 32).

The Apps screen shows the full set of apps on your system (see page 123). The Desktop (see page 44) is where you run standard Windows applications, including Windows Accessories and Microsoft Office applications.

To display the Desktop, select the Desktop tile with the mouse or touch action, or use the WinKey + D keyboard shortcut.

31

Hotspots and Charms

The corners of the Start screen and app screens are hotspots that help you navigate through your Windows 8.1 system.

If you have a Windows 8.1 compliant touchscreen or tablet, you can swipe the edges of the screen to obtain similar effects.

1 Hover the mouse pointer in the lower left corner of the active app screen and the Start icon is displayed. Click to switch to the Start screen

2 From the Start screen, moving to the lower left corner again displays the Start icon. Click to switch to the last active app

3 The Windows key acts as a toggle to switch back and forth between the Start screen and the last used app, or the Desktop if no app has been started

The top and bottom corners on the right will display what's known as the Charms bar (due to its appearance)

1 Move to either hotspot and the charms appear as overlays and not initially active

2 Move the pointer over any of the charms to activate the Charms bar and also display the time and date on the screen

Don't forget

Pressing WinKey + C is another way to display the Charms bar. You can display the Charms bar from any application screen, or from the Desktop.

The final hotspot, at the top left corner, allows you to display the active Windows apps and switch to the one you want.

1 Move to the upper left corner and a miniature of the last active app is displayed. Click to go there

Hot tip

Conventional Windows applications that run on the Desktop are not included, though the Desktop itself appears as an app in its own right.

2 Move the mouse pointer down to display thumbnails for the full list of active apps

3 If you display the app list from an active app, it will show the remaining active apps (plus the Start icon)

4 Hold down WinKey and press the Tab key successively to display the App switcher and to step to each Windows app in turn

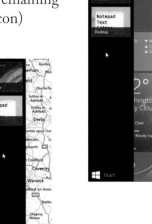

Don't forget

As always, you can use Touch gestures to display and select these lists, if you have the appropriate hardware.

5 Release WinKey to display the last app selected

You can also hold down Alt and press Tab to cycle through the active apps in the standard Windows fashion, showing each app screen in turn.

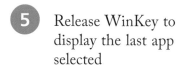

Don't forget

With Alt and Tab, Desktop applications such as Notepad and the Office applications are shown individually.

Don't forget

Though there's no longer a Start menu, there is a useful menu associated with the Start screen icon, providing power user functions.

Beware

The hotspot area at each corner is just a few pixels in size, so it is easy to click the wrong spot and get an unexpected result.

Power Users Menu

There's a menu of useful shortcuts associated with the Start screen thumbnail (see page 32) at the lower left corner hotspot.

1 Display the thumbnail using mouse or touch, then right-click the thumbnail to display the menu

2 Alternatively, press WinKey + X to display that same menu

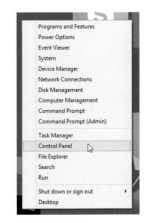

This allows you to access a set of functions that is often needed by the more advanced user, which includes System Properties, Device Manager, Disk Management, Task Manager, Control Panel and File Explorer.

Select Shutdown or sign out, and you can choose to Sign out, Shut down or Restart your system.

Make sure that the Start button is displayed before you right-click or you'll get the right-click action associated with the displayed app. On the Desktop, for example, you might get the Screen menu.

On the Start screen, you'll get the Apps bar (see page 53).

There's a similar Apps bar if you right-click the Apps screen.

Moving Around

If you can see the Windows app you want on the Start screen, left-click the tile with your mouse (or single touch the tile on a touch monitor). To see more tiles and groups, use the scroll bar that appears at the bottom of the screen when you move the mouse. The screen also slides horizontally when you roll the mouse wheel up or down.

You can also use the four keyboard arrows to navigate through the Windows 8.1 apps, then press Enter when the one you want is selected.

Click the Zoom button at the end of the scroll bar and the Start screen contents will be shrunk so you can see all the groups. Click an app or group to reposition the Start screen.

With a Multi-touch monitor or tablet PC, you simply drag the screen to the left or the right as necessary to display other tiles and groups of tiles.

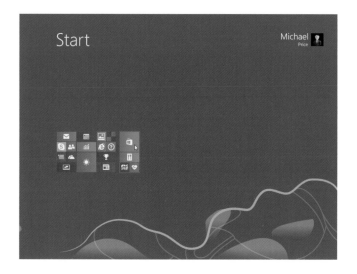

Start an App

Windows apps are represented on the Start screen by tiles. These can display dynamic information from the associated apps, even when they are not running.

Hot tip

With a Windows 8.1 touchscreen or tablet, tap the tile to start the app. With the keyboard, navigate to the required tile using arrow keys and then press Enter.

36

Don't forget

You may be prompted for a response, for example to allow the Weather app to use your actual location.

1. To start an app, move the mouse pointer over the tile for the desired app and left-click to load it

2. The app loads up with a full screen image, in this case weather details for the default location

Close Windows 8.1

The Start button offers one way to close Windows 8.1 (see page 34) but there are several options you can use, some familiar and some new.

Ctrl + Alt + Del

1 Press the Ctrl + Alt + Del key combination

2 Choose Lock, Switch user, Sign out or Task Manager as appropriate

3 Click the Power icon on the lower right and select Sleep (when offered), Shutdown or Restart

Charm Settings

1 Display the Charms bar (see page 32) and select the Settings icon to display Settings

2 Alternatively, you can press WinKey + I to display the Settings pane

3 Click the Power icon to display the Close options and select the one that's appropriate

Hardware Shutdown

On some portable PCs you can close the lid, or press the power button to suspend operations or hibernate the system.

Click the username or picture on the Start screen to Lock or Sign out. Both take you to the Lock screen (see page 28) but Sign out also logs off the user account.

You can also Lock the system using the WinKey + L key combination.

...cont'd

From the Desktop

1 While at the desktop, select a clear area and press Alt + F4 to display Windows Shutdown

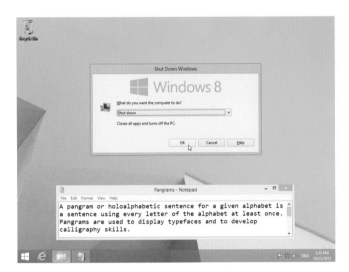

2 Click OK to Shut down, or click the down arrow to list the options that are available

You can choose to:

- Switch User — keep current session and open new
- Sign out — end the current session
- Sleep — save session and set low-power mode (if supported on your computer)
- Shut down — end the session and power off
- Restart — shut down and restart Windows

If an application is selected, pressing Alt + F4 closes that application rather than the desktop.

42

Before choosing Sign out or Shut down from the Desktop, make sure that you save your active applications or documents first.

3 Windows 8.1 Desktop

Although the Start screen has replaced the Start menu, Windows 8.1 still supports the windowed Desktop environment, with taskbar, notification area and Desktop icons and the familiar windows structure, menus and dialogs, and functions for managing Desktop applications.

Display the Desktop

Switch on your computer to start up Windows 8.1 and display the Lock screen (see page 28) and log on to your user account to display the Start screen.

If you are running the Windows RT edition on a tablet PC, this will be your main starting point. For the conventional PC, especially with traditional applications installed, you may prefer to switch to Desktop mode.

There are a number of ways to display the Desktop. For example:

1 Click or touch Desktop on the Start screen or the Apps screen

2 Press the WinKey + D keys

Don't forget

If you have previously displayed the Desktop, you can select it from the Apps switcher (see page 33).

The appearance of your Desktop will vary, depending on configuration and personalization, but you should find:

Desktop Icons   Background Image   Active Task

Start Button   Taskbar Shortcuts   Touch Keyboard   Notification Area

The Touch keyboard appears with touch enabled monitors.

Don't forget

Run a conventional application such as Paint from the Start screen or Apps screen and the Desktop will display with that application open.

...cont'd

The Desktop honors the hotspots and displays the Charms bar, the active app and the Apps switcher. However, the lower left hotspot is replaced by the Start button.

If you tend to use mainly standard Windows applications, you may prefer to start up the computer at the Desktop. You can specify this using Navigation options in Taskbar properties (see page 136).

You can also have the Start button display the Apps screen, and have the Desktop category of applications listed first.

The Desktop itself is displayed via a Windows app and so it has many of the characteristics of the screen for a normal Windows app.

This is particularly useful if you install Microsoft Office, since by default these applications are not pinned to the Start screen or the Taskbar.

With the Apps screen set up this way, it acts very much as a substitute Start menu for Windows applications that run in the Desktop environment. You will also find your Windows apps to the right on the Apps screen, grouped by category.

You can, of course, select all the Office applications you use regularly, and pin them to the Start screen or the Taskbar (see page 69).

Taskbar

The contents of the Taskbar change dynamically to reflect the activities that are taking place on your Desktop.

Taskbar Shortcuts

The right edge of the frame around the task button tells you the number of windows:

Three or more

Two windows

One window

One window

At the left on the Taskbar you'll find the Start button plus shortcuts that turn into task buttons when you select them to start a program. By default, there are shortcuts for Internet Explorer and File Explorer, but you can pin any Windows applications here.

Task Buttons

There is a task button for each open window (program or file folder). The selected or foreground task, in this case the Calculator, is shown emphasized. The other tasks are shaded.

Touch Keyboard

If your system has touch support, you'll find the Touch toolbar which invokes the on-screen keyboard.

Click the button to show hidden icons, in this case for Safely Remove Hardware and Eject Media.

Notification Area

The portion of the bar on the right is known as the Notification Area and contains icons such as Action Center, Network, Speaker and Date/Time. These are system functions that are loaded automatically when Windows starts.

If you have defined more than one input language on your system, you'll have a Language icon which lists the languages installed and makes it easier for you to switch between them.

...cont'd

If you start more tasks, the Taskbar may become full and scrolling arrows will be added to let you select any task.

Hot tip

Taskbar Properties (see page 48) gives options for customizing the location, operation and appearance of the Taskbar.

You can resize the Taskbar, but first it must be unlocked.

1 Right-click an empty part of the Taskbar and, if there's a check next to Lock the Taskbar, click the entry to remove the check and Unlock the taskbar

2 Move the mouse over the edge of the Taskbar until the pointer becomes a double-headed arrow, then drag the border up or down to resize the Taskbar

3 You can lock the Taskbar at the new size – reselect the Lock option from the Taskbar right-click menu

You can add other toolbars to the Taskbar:

1 Right-click an empty part of the Taskbar and select Toolbars

2 Select a toolbar and a tick will be added and the toolbar will be displayed on the Taskbar. Reselect a toolbar to remove it

Don't forget

This right-click menu is also used to arrange windows or to display the Taskbar Properties.

47

Taskbar Properties

To make changes to the Taskbar settings:

1 Right-click an empty part of the Taskbar and select Properties from the menu

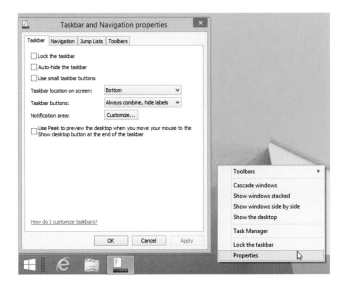

2 Click the Taskbar tab for Taskbar properties

3 You can lock and unlock the Taskbar from Properties as well as from the right-click menu (see page 47)

4 Click the box labelled Auto-hide the Taskbar, to make the full area of the screen available to application windows

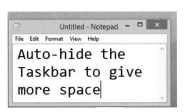

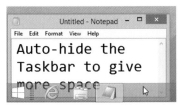

5 It reappears when you move the mouse to the part of the screen where the taskbar should be located

...cont'd

To add shortcuts to the Taskbar or the
Desktop for an existing application:

1 Switch to the Start screen and
type the application name, e.g.
Notepad.exe

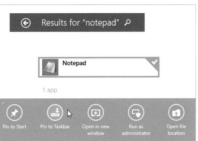

2 Right-click the
result to display
the Apps bar and
click the button to
Pin to Taskbar

3 Switch back to the Desktop and
you'll see the shortcut for the
application on the Taskbar

You can now run the application from the Taskbar. However,
if you prefer you can create the application shortcut on the
Desktop, where there's room for more such shortcuts.

1 Right-click the
shortcut, to display
the Jump List for the
application

2 Right-click the
program name and
click Properties

3 Click the button to
Open File Location,
to open File Explorer
with that file selected

Don't forget

Since you have no
Start menu, you
could add shortcuts
to the Taskbar for the
standard Windows
applications.

53

Don't forget

You can use the
Taskbar entry to locate
the program file and
then create a shortcut
on the Desktop.

...cont'd

Don't forget

If the shortcut does get created within the folder, you can drag and drop it onto the Desktop.

4 In File Explorer, right-click the program file for the application and select Create Shortcut

5 Confirm when prompted that you want the shortcut to be placed on the Desktop

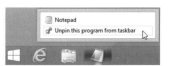

6 You can now run that application from the Desktop by double-clicking the shortcut added there

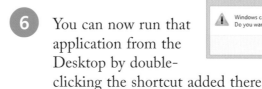

7 To unclutter the Taskbar, right-click the program entry and select Unpin this program from taskbar

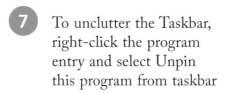

Similarly, you can add other Windows programs such as Paint or Calculator, or applications such as Word and Excel from the Microsoft Office suite.

Hot tip

You may also find that some applications automatically get shortcuts added to the Desktop when installed, for example Abobe Reader.

Window Structure

When you open a folder or start a Windows function or application program on the Desktop, it appears as a window that can be moved and resized. For example:

1 Click the File Explorer shortcut icon on the Taskbar

Not all the Windows applications use the ribbon style. See page 56 for Notepad, an example of a conventional window.

Features of the Window

Quick Access Toolbar

Forward and Back Arrows

Ribbon

Minimize and Maximize Buttons

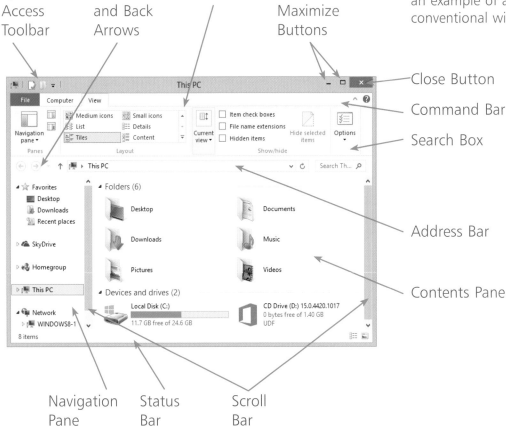

Close Button

Command Bar

Search Box

Address Bar

Contents Pane

Navigation Pane

Status Bar

Scroll Bar

55

2 Click the Maximize button to view the window using the whole screen and the Restore button appears in place of Maximize

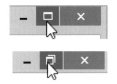

Application Windows

Application programs, even ones included in Windows 8.1, may use the traditional window structure, with Title bar and Menu bar. For example, the Notepad application window:

1 Select Start, All Programs, Accessories and Notepad then type some text (or open an existing file)

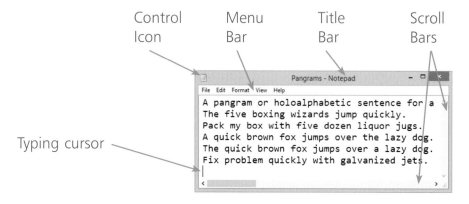

Control Icon   Menu Bar   Title Bar   Scroll Bars

Typing cursor

Other Windows 8.1 applications such as WordPad and Paint use the Scenic Ribbon in place of menu and toolbar.

1 Select Start, All Programs, Accessories and WordPad then open a file (or type some text)

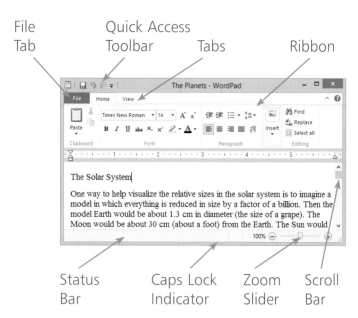

File Tab   Quick Access Toolbar   Tabs   Ribbon

Status Bar   Caps Lock Indicator   Zoom Slider   Scroll Bar

56

Don't forget

Some applications may not use all the features. For example the Calculator window has no scroll bars and also cannot be resized.

Menus and Dialogs

The entries on the Command bars, Menu bars and Ribbons expand to provide a list of related commands to choose. Some entries expand into a submenu, for example:

1 Open the Libraries folder, select Documents and click Manage, then click Set save location. Note the submenu for the Public save location

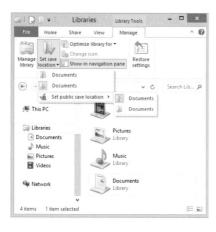

The black triangle opposite a menu entry indicates that there are additional options available to be displayed.

Other entries open dialog boxes that allow you to apply more complex configurations and settings. For example:

1 In the Libraries folder, select the Home tab then click the Properties button

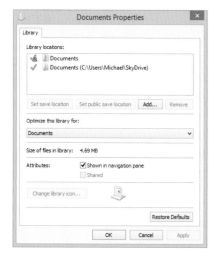

2 The Properties panel is displayed

3 Make changes and click OK to apply, or click Restore Defaults to undo

Some entries are toggles that switch on when selected, then switch off when reselected. For example, a ✓ symbol, may be added to or removed from a box.

Move and Resize Windows

1 To maximize the window, double-click the title bar area (double-click again to restore the window)

2 To move the window, click the title bar area, hold down the mouse button and drag the window

Hot tip

Double-clicking the title bar is an alternative to the Maximize and Restore buttons.

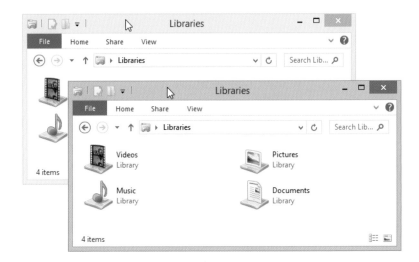

3 To resize the window, move the mouse pointer over any border or any corner

Hot tip

Dragging a corner of the window allows you to adjust the two adjacent borders at the same time.

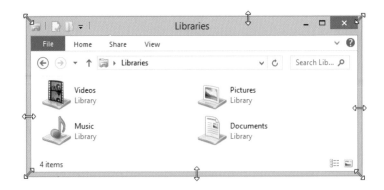

4 When the double-headed resize arrow appears, click and drag until the window is the desired size and in the required location

Snap

On the Windows 8.1 Desktop, the Snap feature offers ways to move and resize windows in one step.

Maximize the Window

1 Drag the title bar to the top of the screen

2 The window's outline expands to fill the whole Desktop

3 Release the title bar to maximize the window

Expand Vertically

1 Drag the top border of the window to the top of the screen

2 The window's outline expands to the height of the Desktop

3 Release the title bar to maximize the height but maintain the width of the window

Compare Two Windows

1 Drag the title bar to the left of the screen

2 Release and the window expands to fill half the Desktop

3 Repeat with a second window, dragging the title bar to the right and you'll be able to view them side-by-side

Don't forget

There is also a Snap function for the Windows 8.1 apps, but this is a simpler function that allows you to view two of the normally full screen apps, side-by-side (see page 38).

Hot tip

You can also drag the bottom border to the bottom edge, to expand vertically.

Hot tip

To return a window to its original size, drag the title bar away from the top of the Desktop and then release.

Close Desktop Apps

When you finish with your active Desktop applications, there are several ways you can close them.

You can also select the application windows and press Alt + F4, or move the mouse over the Taskbar button and click the Close button on the thumbnail.

1 Click the Close button at the top right of the application window

2 Click the Control icon at the left of the title bar and select Close

3 The application may include a File button that offers an Exit option

There are a number of ways to close an application using the Taskbar button that's associated with it.

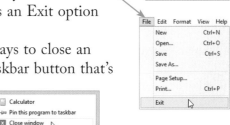

4 Right-click the Taskbar button for the application and select Close window

5 If there are multiple windows for the application select Close all windows

You cannot use the Apps switcher list of active apps (see page 37) to close Desktop apps, even if they were started from one of the Start screen tiles.

6 If any application has a modified document open you'll be prompted to Save changes, whichever method you choose to close your applications

4 Personalize Your System

Change the appearance of the Windows 8.1 Lock screen and Start screen, add an account picture, organize the tiles and the apps, manage your user account, adding picture password or pin code and take advantage of ease of use features. You can also personalize the Desktop environment and manage the display options, including screen resolution and multiple displays.

PC Settings vs Control Panel

Windows 8.1 provides two main ways to make changes to your computer setup and (if you use a Microsoft account to sign on) you can take those changes with you when you sign on at other computers.

Hot tip

The PC Settings app allows you to make a variety of changes to your computer system.

There is a Windows 8.1 function called PC Settings which is an easy way to apply the most often-required changes.

1 Select Settings from the Charms bar (or press WinKey + I) to display the Settings pane

2 Click the button to Change PC Settings

This provides a range of options for you to change the way your system appears or operates and to examine the components that make up your system.

For many users, in particular those with tablet PCs, this will be all that's needed. However, there's a complete set of functions provided via the Control Panel, as in prior releases of Windows, to allow in-depth changes.

Don't forget

Press WinKey + X for the Power Users menu (see page 34) to select Control Panel, or else display the Charms bar on the Desktop and select Settings and then Control Panel.

62

Personalize Lock Screen

The Lock screen appears when you start your Windows 8.1 computer or resume from Sleep. To customize this screen:

1 Select Change PC Settings (see page 62), then click Accounts on the list or click the Lock screen image

2 Click one of the supplied pictures to make it the background image

3 Click Browse to select an image from your Pictures library or another folder

4 Scroll down the Lock screen pane to choose Lock screen Apps to display notifications, updates and alarms

(see page 62)

The Lock screen is full size and includes basic information, such as time and date, plus notifications from various apps.

You can also choose to play the contents of your picture library as a slide show on the Lock screen.

You can have up to seven Windows apps that provide simple status updates, plus a single app to provide more detailed updates.

...cont'd

5 Click one of the existing App icons or Add icon and choose an app from the list (or select Don't show quick status here)

6 Similarly, you can choose the single app that will display detailed status or alarms, (or select the option Don't show... option to remove an existing selection)

You can view the changes without having to wait until the next time you log on to the system. To do this:

1 Switch to the Start screen and right-click the username or the user picture

2 Select Lock to display the Lock screen

Network status   Mail waiting   Meeting notice

Start Screen

1 Display the Charms bar from the Start screen, select Settings and then click Personalize

This allows you to make changes to the color scheme selected during installation, and to choose a background image from the static and animated patterns, solid color, and Desktop wallpaper (to use the same image for Start screen and Desktop).

The pattern is used only for the Start screen, while the background and accent colors will be used in all Windows apps, as well as the Start screen.

1 Click one of the 20 patterns supplied, to make it the background image for the Start screen

2 Drag the sliders to choose the background color and the accent color

3 You'll see the effects on the Start screen, which gets an instant update

If you are signed on with a Microsoft account, your final selection of background image and color will be applied, not just to the current PC, but to any Windows 8.1 PC that you sign on to using the same Microsoft account.

Unlike the Lock screen and the Desktop, the Start screen does not give you the opportunity to choose your own images for the background.

Account Picture

You can specify a photo or image that will be used alongside your username on the Start screen.

1 Right-click the User on the Start screen and select Change account picture, or select Change PC Settings (see page 62), then click Accounts

Don't forget

You can select or create a picture of any size and it will be converted to the appropriate size for use with the Start screen or other functions related to the Microsoft account.

2 Click the Browse button to select an existing image from your Pictures library or another folder

3 Alternatively, if your computer has a webcam or built-in camera, select Camera to take a picture

Beware

You can change the user image from any Windows 8.1 PC, but to remove it completely, you may need to sign on to your Microsoft account using Internet Explorer and amend your profile.

4 You can take a still photo or a video, but the video is limited to five seconds

5 Press the Windows key to toggle between the Settings screen and Start screen, to see the results

If you are signed on with a Microsoft account, the selected image will be displayed on the Start screen of any Windows 8.1 computer that you sign on to. It will also be displayed when you sign on to that account using Internet Explorer, or if you use that account for messaging.

Manage Tiles

The Windows app tiles displayed on your Start screen will depend on the choices made by your supplier and may be in no particular order or sequence, but you do have full control and can add, rearrange and remove as it suits you.

Select Tiles

The first task is to select a tile. You can't just click or touch it, since that will run the associated program. Instead:

1 To select a tile with the mouse, right-click the tile

2 On the App bar displayed, left-click or touch to select the required action, for example Resize

The options offered depend on the particular app selected. For Windows apps such as Finance you can Unpin from Start, Uninstall, Resize and Turn live tile off (or Turn live tile on, if currently off).

You can choose from up to four sizes of tile - three square sizes (Large, Medium and Small) and one oblong size (Wide). For some Windows apps and for Desktop applications, only Medium and Small sizes are offered, e.g.:

3 Select the Maps app and check the Resize options and you'll see just Medium and Small

Hot tip

With a touchscreen, touch and drag down slightly. With the keyboard, use the arrow keys to locate the tile, then press the Spacebar.

Don't forget

If you select and hold a tile, you can drag it into a new position and tiles automatically reflow. This happens also when you Unpin or Resize tiles.

Don't forget

As always, the options offered vary depending on the type of entry selected and its current status.

Hot tip

On the Start screen or the Apps screen, you can select multiple items and apply an action such as Unpin or Resize to all the selected apps at once.

Don't forget

Click the down arrow next to Apps by name, to select a different sequence for display.

| by name |
| by date installed |
| by most used |
| by category |

...cont'd

 4 Select the Windows Store app to see the actions that are offered for this Windows app

The Apps bar displays to offer Unpin from Start, Resize and Turn live tile off. There's no option to Uninstall this app.

Add Tiles

The Apps screen is the usual place to locate apps and add their tiles to the Start screen.

1 At the Start screen, select the Down Arrow, or swipe up the screen to reveal the Apps screen

You'll see all the apps that were installed with your system, listed by name in groups of Windows Apps, Accessories, Ease of Access and System, plus Microsoft Office if installed. Any other apps you have downloaded will also be listed in the appropriate group.

If you have changed Navigation options (see page 136) the Apps screen may display in Categories with Desktop applications listed first.

Manage Apps

Select apps of different types to see what actions are offered:

1 Select a Windows app that's on the Start screen and you can Unpin from Start, Uninstall or Find on Start

Hot tip

The Apps screen lists your applications and allows you to add them to the Start screen or the Taskbar (and create shortcuts on the Desktop – see page 53).

2 For a Windows app not currently on the Start screen, you can Pin to Start or Uninstall

3 Select multiple apps, and you get actions that can be applied to all those apps, plus the Clear selection

Don't forget

You can add items from the Desktop to the Start screen, such as disks, libraries and folders. Right-click the item in File Explorer and select Pin to Start from the menu.

4 Select a Windows accessory such as Paint and you can Pin to Start, Pin to Taskbar, Open new window, Run as Administrator or Open file location

5 If the app is already pinned, you get Unpin and Find

Create a Group

Start screen tiles can be arranged in groups, to bring together sets of related tiles, such as Games or Office applications.

Suppose you pin some Windows accessories and some Office applications to the Start screen. Their tiles will be added at the right, flowing on from the existing tiles.

70

1   To create a group for the Office applications, select all of them and drag them across to the right

Hot tip

As you drag the tile, a bar appears, to show you when to drop the tile to create a group location for that tile.

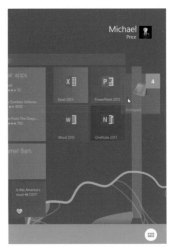

2   When the group separator bar comes into view, release the tiles to create the new group

3 Similarly, select the Windows accessories and drag these to create another group

4 Click the Zoom button at the bottom right of the Start screen, to see the overall view of the groups

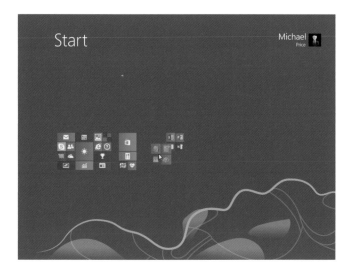

From this view you get the full picture of the apps and their groups, and you can select a group and drag it to change its position relative to the other groups.

Name the Group

1 Right-click the Start screen, and click the Customize button on the Apps bar that is displayed

2 A Name Group header is added to each group on the Start screen

3 Click Name Group for the group you want to name, and a typing area is presented

4 Type a name for the group, e.g. Microsoft Office 2013, and click the Start screen. The group is shown with the name as a header

5 Repeat this procedure to add or change the name for any other groups of tiles you want identified

6 Click the Start screen to remove the Apps bar

Ease of Access

PC Settings also allows you to set up Ease of Access options on your computer, to improve accessibility.

1 In PC Settings, select Ease of Access and review the six categories listed

You'll find help and guidance for using the options in the Ease of Access Center found in the Control Panel (see page 82).

2 Select Magnifier to turn Magnifier on, invert colors and enable tracking (have Magnifier follow the keyboard focus or the mouse cursor)

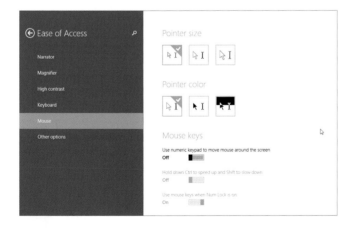

Select Narrator to turn on the screen reader for text and controls, choose a voice, select sounds and manage keyboard and mouse actions.

3 Select Mouse to adjust the pointer size, change the pointer color or use the numeric keypad to move the mouse around the screen

4 You can also manage use of the screen and keyboard

Open Control Panel

For the more comprehensive options for customizing your system, you can use the Control Panel. There are several ways to invoke this:

1 From the Start screen, start typing Control Panel. When the Control Panel entry appears, press Enter

2 From the Desktop, with Show desktop icons enabled (see page 52), double-click the Control Panel icon (if present)

3 From the Desktop, select File Explorer from Taskbar, then This PC, then the Computer tab and select Control Panel from the ribbon

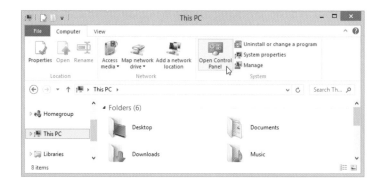

4 From the Desktop, display the Charms bar (see page 32), click Settings and select the Control Panel entry

Note that there's no Control Panel entry for Settings when the Charms bar is displayed from the Start screen, or from any of the Windows apps.

Personalize via Control Panel

When the Control Panel opens, you see the categories as displayed in previous versions of Windows. To personalize:

Control Panel is a Desktop app and so will open as a window on the Desktop.

1 Select the Appearance and Personalization option

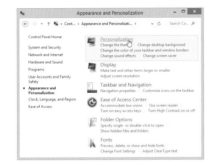

2 Select Personalization to adjust the Desktop

These options will be familiar to users of previous versions of Windows, particularly Windows 7 and Windows Vista. Note that the changes do not affect the Start screen or Windows apps.

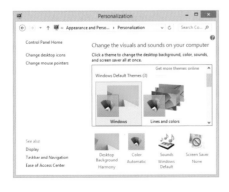

3 Choose a theme or change individual characteristics

Display Settings

Display options other than resolution affect the PC in Desktop mode only and do not affect the Start screen and Windows apps.

You can also right-click the Desktop and select Screen Resolution to show the panel to adjust resolution.

1 From Personalization, select the Display option

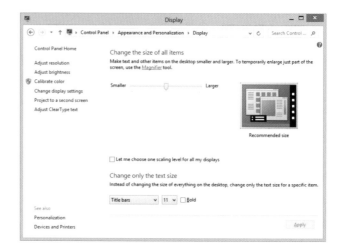

2 You can change the size of text and other items, or you can click Adjust Resolution

3 From here you can set the resolution for your screen, choose the orientation and manage multiple displays

...cont'd

4 Click the down arrow next to Resolution

5 Drag the slider to select a new resolution and click OK

The higher the resolution, the more you can fit on the screen, but the smaller the text and images will then appear.

6 Click the down arrow next to Orientation to select Landscape or Portrait, flipped if desired

7 If you have multiple displays, choose how they'll be used

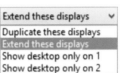

You can duplicate the screen contents, extend to use both, one being the main display, or just use a single screen.

8 After any change, you are asked to confirm that you want to keep the changes, or after a short delay they'll automatically revert to their previous values

You can also control how a projector screen will relate to the PC screen. As with multiple displays, you have the options of duplicating the contents, using the two screens independently or having just one of the screens active.

Beware

The resolutions and color settings offered depend on the type of monitor and the type of graphics adapter that you have on your computer.

Don't forget

A projector can be handled in a similar way to multiple screens attached to the PC.

81

Ease of Access Center

Hot tip

If your PC has a microphone attached, you can use it for Speech Recognition, to dictate to the computer or to issue commands to control the computer.

1 From the Control Panel select the Ease of Access category

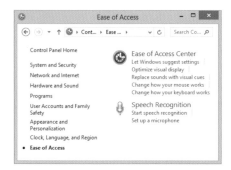

2 For the fullest introduction to the options available, select the Ease of Access Center

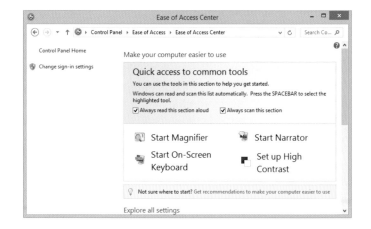

Don't forget

The magnifier is not just for text, it is also very useful for close-up views of images of all types, including graphics, buttons and pictures.

3 Start the main tools – Magnifier, Narrator, On-Screen Keyboard, High Contrast

4 If you are unsure, you can ask for recommendations to make your computer easier to use

5 Scroll down to explore settings, to optimize the computer for limited vision, set up alternatives for input devices and sound and make touch easier to use.

5 Search and Organize

Windows 8.1 helps organize the files and folders on your hard disk. Data is stored by username with separate folders for different types of files, or you can add new folders. Libraries allow you to work with a group of folders. Powerful instant search facilities help you find your way around the folders and the menus.

Files and Folders

The hardware components are the building blocks for your computer but it is the information on your disk drive that really makes your computer operate. There is a huge number of files and folders stored there. To get an idea of how many:

Don't forget

In the Windows 8.1 version of File Explorer, Computer has been replaced by This PC.

1 From the Start screen type Computer and click This PC when that item appears

2 In the File Explorer window that appears, double-click the system drive (C:) to open it

Hot tip

Alternatively, from the Desktop, click the File Explorer icon on the Taskbar and then select the Computer entry on the Navigation pane.

3 Press Ctrl + A to select all the items in the drive

Hot tip

Select the View tab and click the box to Show Hidden items and you'll find there are even more folders on the system hard disk than had initially appeared.

4 Right-click the selection and click Properties

5 This example shows over 66,000 files and 13,000 folders

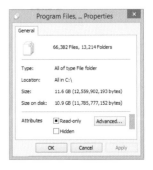

...cont'd

With so many files and folders to handle, they must be well organized to ensure that you can locate the documents, pictures and other data that you require. Windows helps by grouping the files into related sections, for example:

- Program Files   Application programs
- ProgramData   Application data files (usually hidden)
- Windows   Operating system programs and data
- Users   Documents, pictures, etc.

These are top-level folders on your hard disk and each one is divided into subfolders. For example, the Program Files folder is arranged by supplier and application.

1   Open the C: drive, then double-click Program Files, then Adobe and then the Reader subfolders

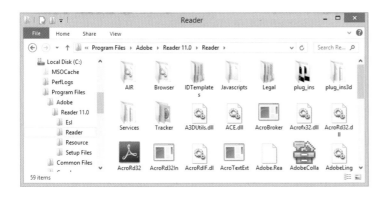

2   Move the mouse pointer over the Navigation pane and you'll see triangles against some folders

3   The white triangle (▷) shows there are subfolders within that folder, and the black triangle (◢) means it is at least partially expanded

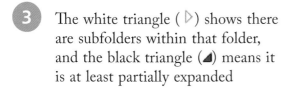

Hot tip

The Users folder contains Documents, Pictures, Music and other folders for each user defined on the computer.

Don't forget

The Program Files, ProgramData and Windows folders are managed by the system and you will not normally need to access them directly.

Hot tip

The triangle symbols also appear when you select any of the folder names within the Navigation pane.

New User Account

Hot tip

Before sharing your PC with other users it is helpful to give them an account of their own with libraries and standard folders.

Don't forget

You can choose to use a local Windows account that is not associated with a Microsoft account (see page 20) but the new users will not be able to download apps and their settings won't travel with them when they switch computers.

Hot tip

For children's accounts you should turn on Family Safety to get reports of their PC usage.

1 Open PC Settings (see page 62) and select Users, then click the button to Add a user

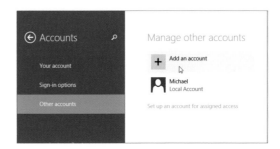

2 Provide an email address for a Microsoft account

3 Click Next and follow the prompts to create the Microsoft account (or access an existing account)

4 The new user is defined to the system, ready for sign in

You can allow a new user to sign in while you are still logged on to the computer.

5 From the Start screen, right-click the username or picture and select the user account required

Alternatively, if you have signed out or shut down the system:

6 From the Logon screen, select the required account, type the password and press Enter

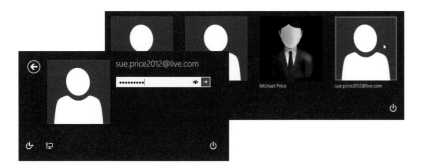

In each case, Windows creates the user libraries and folders (see pages 92-96) and installs any necessary apps. You may be asked to enter a security code to verify the account.

7 When initialization completes, the Start screen appears with the new user account

Hot tip

Any new users that you create are added at the foot of the Users section of PC settings.

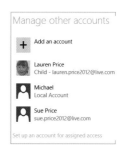

Don't forget

On any subsequent sign in, initialization isn't required so the system goes straight to the Start screen. There's a message if the account has been set up for a child.

Change Account Type

Don't forget

This displays details of all the accounts on your computer. You'll see that the first account created when the system was originally set up has been defined as Administrator.

Hot tip

Note that you cannot create new accounts from within the Control Panel, but must select the link to Add a new user in PC Settings.

Hot tip

Standard user accounts are recommended for every user, even the administrator. To minimize the risk of unintended changes Windows will ask for the administrator password, when that level is needed.

88

1 Select Start, Control Panel and in User Accounts and Family Safety click Change account type

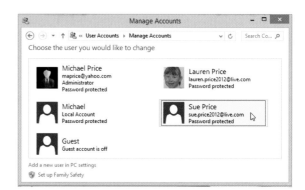

2 Click on one of the new accounts

3 Click Change the account type and you'll see that it has been defined as Standard

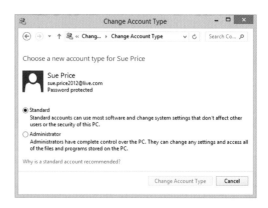

...cont'd

Windows provides a Guest account for casual use, by visitors for example. By default this is turned off. To enable it:

1 Select Change account type from the Control Panel and click on Guest

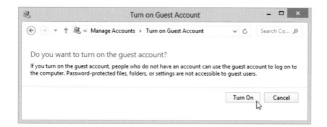

There is no password associated with the Guest account, so anyone with access to your computer can use it. However, they cannot view password protected files, folders or libraries.

2 Click the button to Turn On the Guest account

3 The Guest account is enabled as Local (with no access to the Store)

4 Click Set up Family Safety to see full details and to apply the family safety features to any account

Each account will have its own set of files and folders (see pages 92-96) and also personal preferences such as color themes or backgrounds and password types.

User Folders

Documents and pictures that you create or save on your computer are kept in folders associated with your username.

Don't forget

The Public folder is available to all user accounts and can be used to share files with other people using the same computer or using other computers on the same network. To share with any Internet connected computer or device, you'd use SkyDrive (see page 92),

1 Open the C: drive (see page 84) and double-click the icon for Users

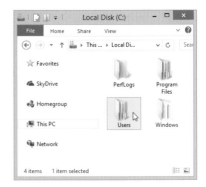

2 There's a subfolder for each user account name defined, plus the Public folder

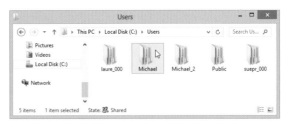

90

Hot tip

To see the hierarchical structure of the user folders, right-click the Navigation pane and select Expand to current folder.

3 Double-click the folder for the active user, in this case Michael Price

There is a set of subfolders with all the documents, pictures, data files and settings belonging to that user. There's also a link to the SkyDrive, the online storage for the user.

Each User folder (including the Public folder) has a similar set of subfolders defined.

The Documents, Music, Pictures and Videos folders can be accessed from This PC in File Explorer, and also from the Libraries link which can be added to the Navigation pane (see page 95xxx).

This PC

This PC in File Explorer is a new feature in Windows 8.1. Like the Computer entry from previous versions that it replaces, it provides a list of the storage devices and drives attached to the local computer.

Hot tip

This PC replaces the Computer entry that you find in File Explorer for previous versions of Windows.

1 Open File Explorer and click This PC

It also replaces (to an extent) the Libraries entries, though this can be reinstated (see page 94).

2 The lower group shows the Devices and drives, in this case the disk drive and the CD drive

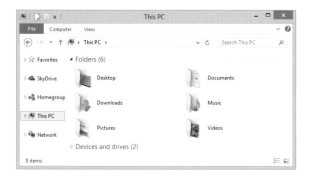

In addition, however, it lists some of the folders associated with the active user.

3 The upper group shows folders for the current user, including Documents, Music, Pictures and Videos (the same folders as used by Libraries)

Don't forget

These are effectively links to the actual folders on the hard disk of the local PC.

4 The Downloads and the Desktop folders are also listed in This PC

SkyDrive

SkyDrive is free cloud storage that comes with your Microsoft account. You can have up to 7GB storage and you can access it from any device where you sign in with your Microsoft account, or from any browser. File Explorer also includes a link to your SkyDrive:

Don't forget

In previous versions of Windows, you needed a Desktop app to access your SkyDrive. In Windows 8.1 you can use File Explorer to transfer files to and from SkyDrive.

1 Open File Explorer and select SkyDrive in the Navigation pane and see the Documents, Pictures, Public and perhaps other folders

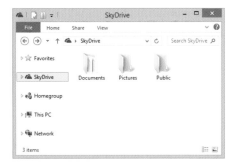

Beware

If you sign in with a local account, the SkyDrive entry does not appear in File Explorer.

2 Select View and choose Details from the Layout group

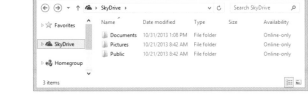

3 You'll find that, by default, the folders are available online only, so you cannot open or save files on the SkyDrive unless connected

If you sometimes work offline, for example while traveling but still need particular files, you can choose to make them available offline. Any changes that are made while you are disconnected will be automatically synced the next time you are online. To work offline with SkyDrive files:

1 Locate and select the files you want, then right-click them and select Make available offline

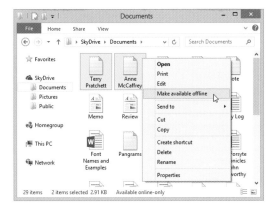

Hot tip

You can select a folder to make all its files available offline, or the SkyDrive entry itself to make all files available offline.

93

2 Switch to the Details view for the folder containing the files and you'll see they are now Available offline

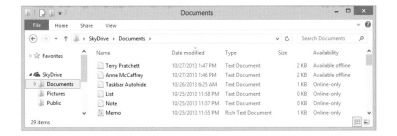

3 To check the status of your SkyDrive, open PC Settings and click the SkyDrive entry

Don't forget

The SkyDrive section of PC Settings tells you how much SkyDrive storage you have used, allows you to purchase more, and lets you choose to save documents to SkyDrive by default.

Libraries

Libraries contain pointers to individual folders but allow you to treat the contents as if they were all in one folder. Typically the Documents library would be a combination of the user's Documents folder and the Public Documents folder. This allows you to share documents with others (or share their documents). In Windows 8.1, Libraries are not displayed by default, but you can add them to File Explorer.

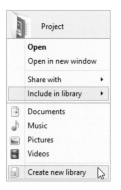

You can right-click any folder on your hard drive or SkyDrive, select Include in library, and add it to one of the four libraries, or use it to create a new library.

1 Open File Explorer, right-click the Navigation Pane and select Show libraries

By default, your SkyDrive is used for sharing documents, though you can revert to the local Public folders if you share files on your local area network only.

2 Select the Libraries entry that gets added, and you'll see the expected four libraries – Documents, Pictures, Music and Videos

3 Double-click the Documents library and you'll see it has files from two locations – the user's Documents folder and the SkyDrive Documents folder

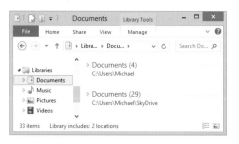

Folder Navigation

When you open a drive or folder, you'll find a number of different ways to navigate among the folders on your disk.

1 Open the Documents folder in File Explorer

Quick Access Toolbar   Tab Bar   Title Bar   Search Box

Forward, Back

Up One Level

Address Bar

Navigation Pane

Contents Pane

Details Pane

Status Bar

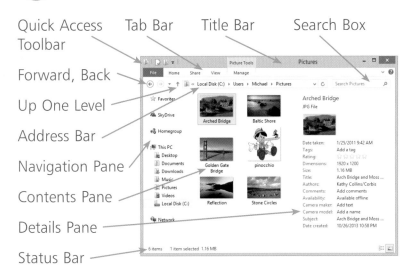

Hot tip

Click the Forward and Back buttons to navigate through locations you have already visited.

2 To go directly to a location on the Address bar, just click that location, for example the User's folder (in this case Michael)

3 To go to a subfolder of a location on the Address bar, click the arrow at the right, and select a subfolder from the list displayed

Don't forget

The address bar displays the current location as a series of links, separated by arrows. There's an Up arrow at the left, to go Up one level.

4 To type a location, click the blank space to the right of the current location

5 The current folder address is displayed, highlighted

6 Edit the folder address to the required location, for example C:\Users\Public\Pictures and then press Enter to go to that location

Hot tip

For common locations, you can type just the name, for example:
- Computer
- Contacts
- Control Panel
- Documents
- Pictures

Create Folders and Files

Create new folders
to organize all your
documents by use or
purpose, or create files
of particular types,
ready for use.

1 Open the library or folder where the new folder is
required, for example select Libraries, Documents

2 Right-click an empty part of the folder area and
select New > Folder (or choose a particular file type)

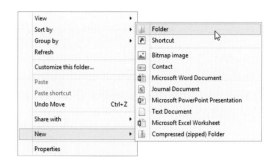

Choose one of the
file types, for example
Microsoft PowerPoint
Presentation, and
it will be initially
named as New
Microsoft PowerPoint
Presentation. Overtype
this name, as shown
for the New Folder.

3 Overtype the name New folder with the required
name and press Enter (or click elsewhere)

If you create a folder or a file in a library such as Documents
or Pictures, it will be created and stored within the library's
default save location, for example the current user's My
Documents or My Pictures.

Copy or Move Files

You can copy a file or files using the Windows clipboard.

1 Open the folder containing the file, right-click the file icon and select Copy (to record the file path)

2 To copy multiple files, use Shift or Ctrl to select multiple files before clicking Copy

3 Locate and open the destination folder, right-click an empty space and select Paste to store a copy of the file in that folder

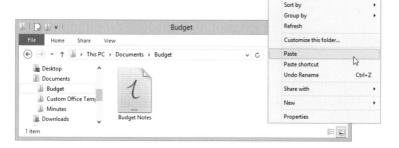

4 To move a file to the new location rather than make a copy, right-click the file icon and choose Cut

Budget 2013

5 The original file icon will be dimmed until you select Paste, when it will be transferred to the new location

Budget 2013

Hot tip

You could also select the file or files and then press the keyboard shortcut Ctrl + C for Copy.

Hot tip

Alternatively, select the folder and then press the keyboard shortcut Ctrl + V for Paste.

Hot tip

The keyboard shortcut is Ctrl + X to Cut the selected files.

...cont'd

To move or copy files using drag-and-drop operations:

1 Use File Explorer to locate and open the folder with the files you want to move

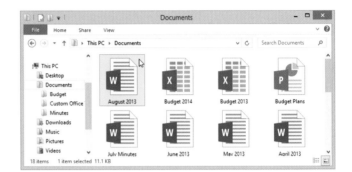

2 Select the first file then press the Ctrl key as you select the second and subsequent files

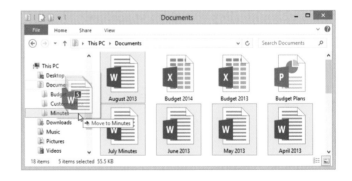

3 Click and hold any of the selected files, then drag the selection to the target folder and release there

4 To Copy rather than Move the files, hold down Ctrl as you drag and release the selection

5 If the target folder is in a different drive, hold down Shift as you drag to Move, otherwise you will Copy

Using the Search App

Windows 8.1 includes a Smart Search that integrates the facilities of Bing and searches everywhere for matches.

1 Search from the Start screen by just typing the text terms

2 Relevant results are displayed. Press Enter for the full results

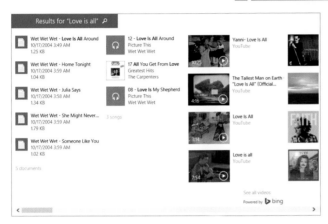

3 You'll find results from files on your hard disk, videos on YouTube and links to many websites. You also get data from related apps. A search for London, for example, shows Weather as well as many useful links

In Windows 8, Search from the Start screen looked only at Apps, the default category. Search selected from the Charms bar would use a category appropriate to the particular app.

If there's too much information, click the arrow next to Everywhere and choose a specific category of data.

Settings for Search App

1. Open the Charms bar and click Settings (or press WinKey + I to display the Settings pane)

2. Click the button to Change PC Settings then click Search and apps, and select Search

Hot tip

Windows will save your searches as future suggestions. However, you can choose to clear search history, perhaps to avoid displaying confidential details.

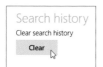

Don't forget

If you disable use of Bing, searches Everywhere will exclude web images and web videos.

3. Enable or disable the use of Bing to search online

4. Choose whether to allow personalized results from Bing, and whether to allow use of your location

5. Adjust the level of safe search filtering you want applied to web results

6. Control how Bing operates while your system is accessing the Internet via a metered connection

6 Desktop Applications

Windows 8.1 includes some useful Desktop applications for calculating, text editing, word processing and picture editing and you can search the Internet for external programs to handle other functions.

Conventional Applications

Windows 8.1 provides the operating environment for a variety of applications. In many cases, these are supplied as separate programs or suite of programs. However, some of the desired functions may be in the form of small but potentially very useful programs included with Windows and known as Windows accessories. The main application areas and the related Windows programs are:

Don't forget

These applications take advantage of Windows 8.1 features and can be pinned to the Start screen, but they do not operate as Windows apps (see page 36).

- Text processing   Notepad
- Word processing   WordPad
- Electronic mail   [see chapter 8]
- Drawing   Paint
- Spreadsheet   Calculator only
- Database   [no program]
- Multimedia   [see chapter 11]

Don't forget

You can change the Navigation options (see page 136) to display the Apps screen in Category order, with the Desktop applications listed first.

For requirements that are not supported by the programs in Windows, you'll need to install separate programs or a suite of programs such as Adobe Acrobat or Microsoft Office. Even if you don't have these you may need readers and viewers, free programs that allow you to view the files created by those separate applications. You can also install Desktop apps from the Windows Store (see page 134).

Calculator

While no substitute for a spreadsheet application, Windows Calculator provides quite powerful computational facilities.

1 Select Start, All Programs, Accessories, Calculator

2 Type or click to enter the first number, the operation symbol and the next number

3 Enter any additional operators and numbers and press = to end

Click the calculator buttons or press the equivalent keyboard keys, to perform Add, Subtract, Multiply, Divide, Square Root, Percent and Inverse operations. You can also store and recall numbers from memory and the History capability keeps track of stages in the calculations.

Scientific, Programmer and Statistics views are also provided:

1 Open Calculator, select View and choose, for example, Scientific

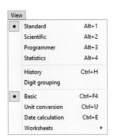

The Scientific calculator includes a variety of functions and inverse functions, including logarithms and factorials.

Windows Calculator also supports unit conversions, date calculations and some basic worksheet functions for mortgage, vehicle lease and fuel economy calculations.

You can also use the numeric keypad to type numbers and operators. Press Num Lock if it is not already turned on.

A Windows app Calculator is also included. You'll find this on the Apps screen.

You will find other, specialized calculators in the Windows app format, if you Search the Windows Store.

Notepad

Notepad is a text editor that you can use to create, view or modify text (.txt) files. It provides only very basic formatting and handles text a line at a time.

Don't forget

The absence of formatting turns into a benefit when you are working with the source files for a program or the HTML code for a web page, since these require pure text.

Hot tip

Edit, Go To and type a line number to go to a specific line in the file (as shown in the Status bar).

Beware

The Go To function is grayed and disabled and the Status bar is hidden when you select the Word Wrap option.

1 Search for Notepad at the Start screen and select the program, then type some text, pressing Enter for each new line

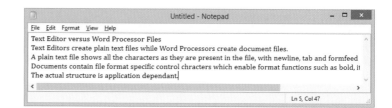

2 Select File, Save As and type the required file name (with file type .txt) then click Save

3 To show the whole of the long text lines in the window, select Format and click Word Wrap

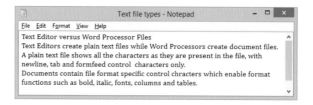

4 When you print the file, it will wrap according to the paper width, regardless of the word-wrap setting

WordPad

WordPad also offers text-editing, but adds tools and facilities for complex formatting of individual pieces of text.

1 Find and start the WordPad program and enter text, pressing Enter to start each new paragraph

2 Use the formatting bar to change the font, size, style and color for selected (highlighted) text

3 Click the Save button on the Quick Access Toolbar (or press Ctrl + S)

WordPad uses the ribbon rather than a menu bar. There are two tabs: Home and View. The File button provides Save, Setup and Print functions.

Click the left, center or right alignment button to adjust the positioning of the selected paragraph or line of text.

Save WordPad documents as .rtf (Rich Text Format) to retain the text formatting. Saving as .txt will remove the formatting (and images or links).

Insert Pictures

WordPad also allows you to include pictures in documents.

You can also click the Paint drawing button, to insert a drawing that you create using Microsoft Paint.

1 Position the typing cursor and click the Insert, Picture button on the Home tab

2 Locate and select the picture and click Open

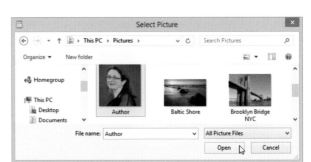

Don't forget

WordPad can open text files in a variety of formats, including Open XML, Unicode Text and Microsoft Office .docx (but not the older .doc format).

Rich Text Format (*.rtf)
Office Open XML Document (*.docx)
OpenDocument Text (*.odt)
Text Documents (*.txt)
Text Documents - MS-DOS Format (*.txt)
Unicode Text Documents (*.txt)
All Wordpad Documents (*.rtf, *.docx, *.odt, *.txt)
All Documents (*.*)

3 A copy of the image is added to the document and displayed at the cursor location

4 If it's the wrong size, right-click the picture, select Resize picture and choose the scale required

Paint

Paint is a digital sketchpad that can be used to draw, color and edit pictures. These can be images that you create from scratch, or you can modify existing pictures, such as digital photographs or a web page graphics. For example:

1 Select Paint from the Apps screen, to start up with a blank canvas

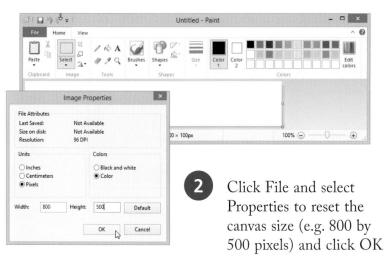

2 Click File and select Properties to reset the canvas size (e.g. 800 by 500 pixels) and click OK

3 Select the arrow below Paste, select Paste From, locate a picture to add to the canvas and click Open

4 Drag the image to position it

...cont'd

Hot tip

Draw a second frame and use the Fill tool to color the space between the frames.

5 Select the Rounded Rectangle tool then click and drag to draw a frame around the picture

6 Use the Text tool to draw a text box and add information such as a description of the contents

7 To make changes, select the View tab and the Zoom in button, or the View tab and the Magnifier

Don't forget

Choose a suitable file type such as .jpeg for pictures, or .png for documents. Paint also supports .bmp, .gif and .tif file formats.

8 When you've finished changes, select File, Save, type the file name and click Save

Unknown File Types

Windows and its applications cannot help when you receive attachments or download files of unknown file types.

1 If there are unknown file types in your Downloads folder, the extensions (normally hidden) are displayed

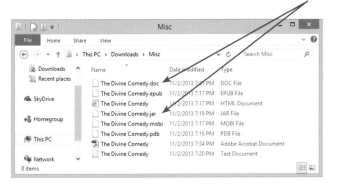

2 Double-click an unknown type, e.g. Solar System.doc, and you are asked how you want to open it

3 Click More options to view suggested programs. If none are suitable, select Look for another app on this PC

4 Otherwise you can Look for an app in the Store

Don't forget

You can also right-click the file and select Open with, to get the list of suggestions.

Hot tip

If there's nothing suitable, just press Escape. Anything you choose gets remembered, even if it doesn't work for that file type.

Beware

In previous releases, Windows offered a Web service to look for suitable programs. If the Store does not find a good answer, you could search the Internet yourself (see page 118).

Search Web for Software

FilExt is a free online service by UniBlue, the PC Tools supplier. They, of course, take the opportunity to remind you about their products.

If there's no obvious choice from the Windows suggestions, you can search on the Internet for suitable software.

1 To get information about the use and purpose of an unknown file type go to **FilExt at http://filext.com**

The .doc extension has been used by many programs over the years. Microsoft Word is the most likely entry in this case.

2 For Doc file extension, select letter D from the index and scroll down to locate entries for .DOC

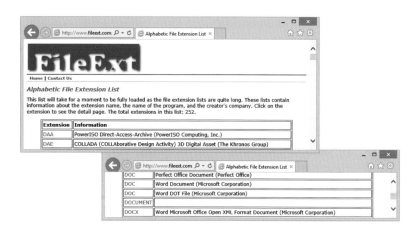

3 Select the most appropriate entry, e.g. Word Document (Microsoft Corporation)

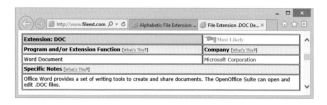

...cont'd

4 Select the link to open the Microsoft website and search for Word Viewer

Microsoft also provides free viewers for other Office applications including Access, Excel, PowerPoint and Visio.

5 Follow the links to Download and Run the Setup program, accept the terms and Install Word Viewer

An entry for Microsoft Office Word Viewer is added to the Apps screen (but by default it is not pinned to the Start screen).

6 When installation completes, the .doc files are recognized and will open in Word Viewer

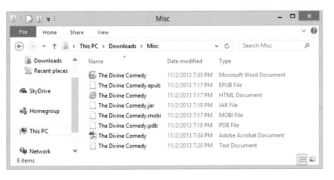

119

Change Default Program

With Word Viewer installed, you now have two programs that can load Rich Text Format documents. To review the options and confirm the default program for .rtf files:

1 Right-click any .rtf file and select Open With to list the programs available on your system

2 Both WordPad and Word Viewer are shown

3 Select the box Use this app for all .rtf files, then click WordPad

4 The icons for the files indicate that the .rtf file uses WordPad as default, the .doc file uses Microsoft Word Viewer, while the .txt file uses Notepad

7 Windows Apps

The emphasis is on the new full screen Windows 8.1 functions. Some, such as Reader and SkyDrive, are supplied at installation time. However, there are many Windows apps at the Windows Store, where you search, review descriptions, then download and install apps on your system.

In the past, Windows applications have been available from many sources, including supplier and enthusiast websites, as well as Microsoft. Sources for Windows apps are much more limited.

122

All Windows apps must be submitted to Microsoft for certification before they are allowed in the Windows Store (or included on installation discs).

Sources for Apps

Although desktop and conventional applications are supported (see page 44), the main functions are provided by the new-style Windows apps. As already discussed, these are full screen programs, except when Windows Snap allows two or more apps to share the screen.

The primary design point for the Windows app is the touchscreen as exemplified by the tablet PC, but all the apps can also be operated on a system with standard monitor, mouse and keyboard equipment.

The Window apps that are available can be found in just two places:

1   Supplied and installed with Windows 8.1

This is a typical Start screen for a newly-installed Windows 8.1 system, showing some of the Windows apps you may expect to find installed.

2   For Download and Install from the Windows Store

The range of Windows apps available at the Windows Store can be expected to change frequently, as new products are added and others removed or revised.

Programs submitted to Microsoft can also include Desktop apps. These are conventional applications that are listed at the Windows Store, but provided from the manufacturer's website, via a link that is included with the application description. These and other conventional apps may still be obtained directly, without visiting the Windows Store.

Supplied with Windows 8.1

The details may change with updates to Windows 8.1, or with customization by your computer supplier, but these are the Windows apps that were initially included on the installation disc, as displayed on the Apps screen.

From the Start screen, swipe up or click the Down arrow to display the Apps screen.

On the Apps screen, swipe up or click the Up arrow to return to the Start screen.

123

There are 29 Windows apps shown on the initial Apps screen. By default, 22 of these have Tiles on the Start screen. There are seven that do not usually appear (Alarm, Calculator, Health & Fitness, PC Settings, Reader, Scan and Sound Recorder).

There are four different sizes of tile available, and you can select the size you prefer. The Large and Wide options are particularly suitable for Live tiles that display real-time information. However, some Windows apps are restricted to Medium and Small options.

To change the tile size, right-click and select Resize from the Apps bar then choose the desired size from the list that appears.

Some of these apps, such as Mail, Internet Explorer, Music, Photos and Video, will be discussed in the relevant chapters on the specific topics.

On the following pages we will look more closely at the Reader and some of the other apps.

Reader

This is Microsoft's own Windows app for reading Adobe PDF (Portable Document Format) files. It isn't normally added to the Start screen, so to start the app:

1 Display the Apps screen and touch or click the entry for Reader

2 The first time you start Reader, it tells you there's no recent history and suggests you browse for files

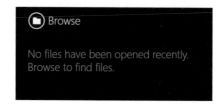

Don't forget

Reader does not have a tile on the Start screen, since it is usually started automatically. However, you can Pin to Start if you wish.

3 It suggests your SkyDrive (see page 126), but you can browse your computer, Homegroup or network

4 In future, it will remember the last document viewed and open that one

More typically, you might come across a PDF file while checking your folders and decide to view that file.

1 Double-click the PDF file (or select and press Enter)

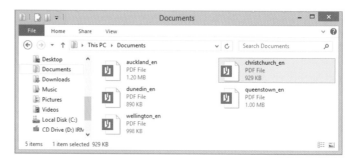

2 If not already active, the Reader app is launched

Hot tip

Reader is designed to handle Adobe's PDF files and the Microsoft equivalent, XPS files.

...cont'd

3 The PDF is loaded with the first page displayed

4 Right-click the screen to display the App bar

5 Find text, or select Two page or One page view

6 Click More to Rotate the document or get Info. You can annotate and Save the PDF

You can Zoom the picture by using the Stretch action on a touch system, using Crtl + - or Ctrl + =, with Ctrl + mouse wheel, or by clicking the - and + buttons.

By default, Reader uses continuous display and scrolls vertically, but you can select full page views and scroll horizontally.

The App bar also provides the option to Print the PDF (or XPS) file.

SkyDrive

Microsoft SkyDrive is a file hosting service that allows you to upload and sync files to a cloud storage facility and then access them from a Web browser or your local computer (or other device). It allows you to keep your files private, or share them with your contacts, or make the files public.

This service offers 7GB of free storage for new users. Additional storage is available for purchase. Files of size up to 2GB can be stored in your SkyDrive folders. (*Correct at the time of printing.*)

To access your SkyDrive:

Hot tip

You need to be signed in with your Microsoft account to access your SkyDrive. To access a SkyDrive belonging to a different account, you must use your web browser and the **SkyDrive.com** website.

1 Switch to the Start screen and click the SkyDrive tile

2 The application launches

3 Your SkyDrive is displayed, showing the top level folders

Don't forget

You can also access your SkyDrive from File Explorer (see page 84) and from within many Desktop applications and Windows apps.

4 The first time you run the SkyDrive app, you are offered information about SkyDrive. Press Close and then select a folder, e.g. Pictures

...cont'd

5 The Pictures folder is displayed in Thumbnail view

Right-click the App window to display the App bar with the options Select all, New Folder and Add files (upload from your PC drive).

6 Click the Details button to switch to the file view, and the button is replaced by the Thumbnail button

Select a file to open it in the associated application, for example .txt files in Notepad. However, you need to go to **SkyDrive.com** if you want to view Office documents using the Office Web Apps.

7 Right-click to select a file or folder and a more comprehensive App bar is displayed, including options to Delete, Copy, Rename, Make offline, etc.

Windows Store Categories

The Windows Store recognizes your system and displays apps that are appropriate. To see what you'll be offered:

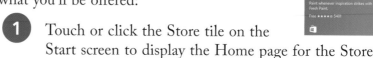

The Windows Store for Windows 8.1 systems is arranged in various groupings, to help you explore its contents and find apps that are useful to you.

1 Touch or click the Store tile on the Start screen to display the Home page for the Store

2 Scroll vertically to review the spotlighted apps on the left hand side

3 Scroll horizontally for groups of apps: Picks for you; Trending; New & Rising; Top paid; Top free

Each Windows 8 App is assigned to a specific category. It may also appear in the Spotlight list or one of the five Home page groups, but it won't be found under any other category.

4 Right-click the Store screen to list all the groups

In addition to the five groups shown on the Home page there are 20 different categories of app listed.

Books & Reference

You can use the categories to explore the Store's contents:

1 Select a category of interest, e.g. Books & Reference

For each category you can expect to see spotlight apps and groups such as New & Rising, Top paid and Top free, plus a link to See all.

2 Scroll the screen to find the See all link on the right

To help locate apps of interest you can filter the results by Subcategory or Price and choose a suitable Sort sequence.

3 Click See all to display the full list for the category

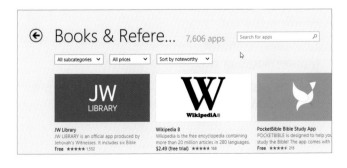

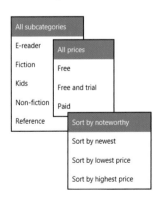

Search Windows Store

You can use the Search box found on every Windows Store screen to view its scope and find items of interest.

1 Select the Search box and type the search term, e.g. Books

2 The top matches are displayed and similar searches are listed

3 Click the spyglass icon to show all the results

Sort by relevance
Sort by newest
Sort by highest rating
Sort by lowest price
Sort by highest price

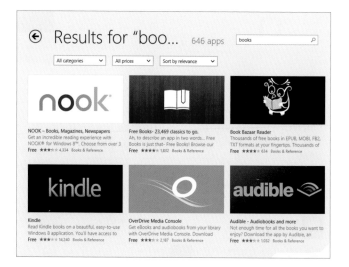

4 Click All prices and select Paid, to list those apps

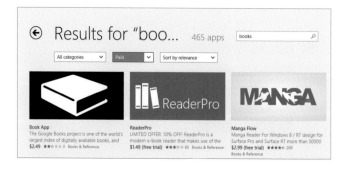

Installing Apps

1 Find an app you want to review, for example Free Books

2 Click the Install button if you want this app on your system

3 Messages at the Store show you the installation in progress and completed

4 Go to the Apps screen to run the new app (or to Pin to Start)

If you've installed the app on another PC (using the same Microsoft account) you'll be reminded.

You'll be told if the app is already installed on the current PC.

Your App Account

From Windows Store you can check your account and see what apps you have installed, even if you use your Microsoft account on multiple machines.

1 Right-click the Store screen and select Your account

2 You can add credit card details for when you buy apps, and check the PCs assigned to your account

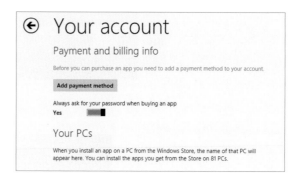

3 Right-click the screen and select Your apps

4 Click Select all, or right-click individual apps and then click Install, to add the apps to the current PC

Beware

You can install apps from the Store, free or charged, on up to five Windows 8.1 or Windows 8 systems. You can remove computers that are no longer used, to allow for new computers.

Don't forget

Your apps determines all the apps installed on PCs assigned to your Microsoft account and lists the apps not installed on this PC.

Updates

If any Windows apps that you've installed get updated, the changes are provided by the Windows Store. In Windows 8.1 these updates are applied automatically in the background, and you get no notification.

If you'd prefer to know what's happening:

1 Open the Windows Store, display the Charms bar and select App updates

Hot tip

When you turn off automatic updates for apps, you'll get notifications on the Store tile and on the Store screen, just as with Windows 8.

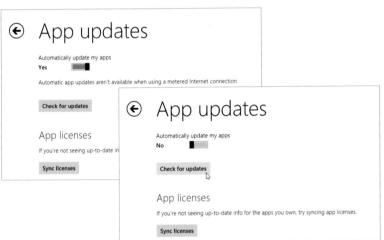

2 Click the button to turn off automatic updates. You can then revisit App updates periodically and select Check for updates

The updates will be preselected, but you can right-click to deselect any you don't want to install at this time. Click Install to begin applying the selected updates.

Don't forget

You'll see progress reports as the updates are applied, saying Pending, Downloading and Installing.

Desktop Apps

Windows Store includes entries for Desktop apps, which are conventional Windows applications that run in the traditional Desktop environment.

There's no explicit search for Desktop apps – you'll just come across them during your searches for Windows 8 apps. For example:

1 Search the Windows Store using the term Desktop to get 1000 apps

Hot tip

You cannot purchase Desktop apps from the Windows Store – it just provides a link to the publisher's website.

2 Examine the results and you'll see Desktop app, rather than the price (or Free)

3 Filter by Price, and you'll find a spattering of Desktop apps in Free, Free and Trial and Paid apps

Hot tip

1000 is the maximum number for results from the Store in Windows 8.1, but filtered lists in this example show:
Free   797
Free and trial 886
Paid   314

A scan of the results suggests there are hundreds of Desktop apps. However, this is not an exclusive search.

134

Install Desktop Apps

To illustrate installation of Desktop apps:

1 Select the free Desktop app Pinger

2 Review the details at the Store

Hot tip

You cannot rely on the Price category for Desktop apps in the Windows Store – you must check the terms and conditions at the publisher's website.

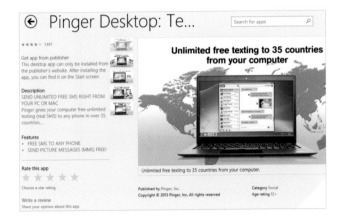

3 Select Get app from publisher, and the website displays on a shared screen (you can go full screen)

Hot tip

When the example Desktop app is installed, an icon is added to the Desktop, but the app is not pinned to Start or to the Taskbar.

4 Follow the prompts to download and run the setup program and install the Desktop app

Start Up at Desktop

If you are using mainly conventional Windows applications you may prefer to start up at the Desktop rather than the Start screen. Windows 8.1 provides options for this.

1 Switch to the Desktop, right-click the Taskbar and select Properties

2 On the Taskbar and Navigation properties, click the Navigation tab and select your preferred settings

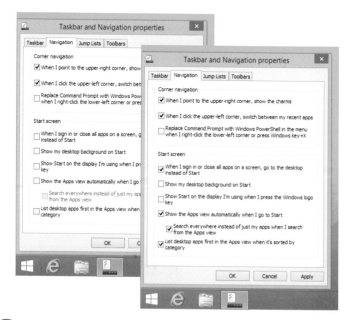

3 For example, you might choose to go to the Desktop when you sign in or to show the Apps screen instead of the Start screen when you select the Start button or the Windows Logo key

Don't forget

You can revert to a mode of operation that is more like the previous versions of Windows, but using the Apps screen rather than the Start menu for selecting applications.

Hot tip

You can disable the hotspots (see page 32) on the upper left and right corners, if you don't want to display the Charms Bar or the Apps Switcher.

Hot tip

You can also choose to search everywhere instead of just your apps when you use the Search box on the Apps screen, and to list Desktop apps first on the Apps screen.

8 Email and Calendar

Windows 8.1 provides the Mail app for email communications, the People app to manage the details of your contacts and the Calendar app to keep track of events and meetings. Communicate instantly using the Skype app. For services such as POP mail, you can use Outlook from Office 2013.

An email address consists of a username or nickname, the @ sign and the server name of your email provider, e.g. jsmith99@myisp.com or web service e.g. jsmith99@gmail.com.

Hot tip

The Mail, Calendar and People apps are packaged together, though Messaging is now handled separately handled by the Skype app.

Electronic Mail

Email or electronic mail is used to send and receive text messages. You can send an email message to anyone with an email address, you can receive messages from anyone who knows your email address and you can reply to those messages, or forward them to another email address. You can send your email message to more than one person at the same time and attach files such as documents or pictures.

Email is free, since no stamp or fee is required. However, before you can use email, you require:

- An account with an Internet Service Provider (ISP)
- An Internet connection such as telephone or cable
- A modem or router to make the connection
- An email address from your email service provider or from a web service such as Gmail or Hotmail
- An email program such as Mail or Outlook 2013

Mail
This is the Windows app that is installed along with Calendar and People, when Windows 8.1 is set up. It provides full screen access to multiple email accounts.

Outlook 2013
This is one of the applications included with Microsoft Office 2013, and is installed with Windows RT 8.1 and with Windows 8.1 systems that have Office 2013 added. It provides full function email and time management services, and runs on the Desktop as a windowed application.

Other Email Programs
A recent search at the Windows Store for Email Clients found 105 apps (including 71 free apps and 11 Desktop apps. They cover many specialized interests and some of them resolve limitations of the Mail app, e.g. POP mail.

View Message

1 Select a message in the Folder pane and it displays in the Reading pane

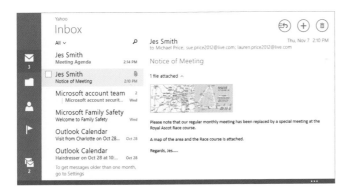

Pictures can be embedded in the message. Other files such as documents can be saved or opened from the message.

2 If there is an attachment (as indicated by a Paperclip icon) it will be embedded or shown as a link

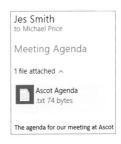

3 Click the Respond button and select Reply (to sender), Reply all or Forward to another person

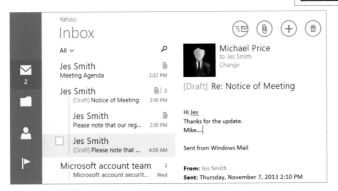

You can add people from your Contacts list (see page 148) and you can also switch the account used to send the reply.

4 Type your reply and click the Send button when finished

5 A copy is saved in the Sent folder for the account used to send the reply

People

Windows 8.1 allows you to collect details of all your contacts and make them available to apps such as Mail and Calendar, using the new People app.

Don't forget

The People app can manage all contacts associated with your email and personal networking, but you need to define which accounts to use.

1 Click the People tile on the Start screen

Hot tip

Click the Connected to bar at the foot of the window and the Accounts pane will be displayed immediately.

2 Display the Charms bar and select Settings and then Accounts

3 To start with there may be just your Microsoft account, which may initially have no contacts list associated with it

Hot tip

LinkedIn is used as an example, but you'd follow a similar procedure for any of the account types.

4 Click Add an account

5 Identify the types of account that have contacts that you may want to add

6 For example, choose the LinkedIn account

...cont'd

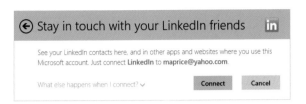

7 Click Connect for your LinkedIn account

8 To grant access, enter your Email and Password for LinkedIn and click OK, I'll Allow It

9 Type the words as displayed (case doesn't matter) to validate the request and click Continue

10 LinkedIn will be added to the connected accounts

Don't forget

To change the access settings, select Settings and Accounts and click the new account.

Select Manage this account online, and Internet Explorer opens to give you the option to change or remove the connection.

Hot tip

The codes are not always easy to read, but you can click the buttons to display a new code or to request an audio prompt.

Viewing Contacts

The People app adds details of the contacts in your account.

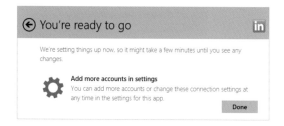

Syncing...

1 Switch to People and click a letter to view the details

2 Using Windows 8.1 Snap, you can view your contacts beside another app such as Mail

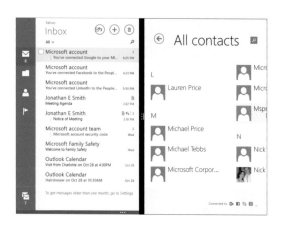

Managing Contacts

1 From the People app, select Settings from the Charms bar and click Options

2 Click the button to sort your contacts by last name, if desired

3 Hide contacts from some of your accounts, to reduce the number being displayed

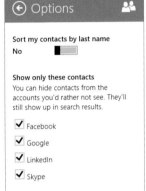

4 To work with a specific contact, click the entry

If you right-click the Contacts page and select New from the App bar, you can enter the details for a new contact.

New contact

5 You can send an email, make a phone call, map the contact's address or view more info

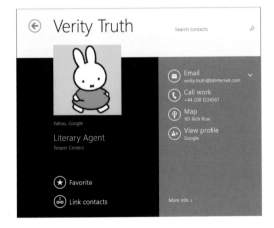

If you Edit the contact details, your changes will be shared with the originating account, the next time you Sync Mail and Contacts.

6 Assign the contact as a Favorite, or right-click the details page to display the App bar where you can Pin to Start, Edit the contact's details, or Delete a contact that's no longer needed.

Create a Message

Don't forget

You can alternatively select the recipient from People and click Send Email (see page 147).

Hot tip

You can also click the People icon to display your Favorites list, or browse your contacts in the People app, displayed alongside the Mail app.

1 Select the email account, go to the Inbox and click New (or press Ctrl + N)

2 A blank message form is displayed, ready for typing

3 Begin typing the contact name in the To box, then select the contact when it appears

4 Add other recipients and Cc (Carbon-copy) recipients as required

5 Type the Subject for the message

6 Add the greeting and the message text

7 End with your name and the email signature for the sending account

8 Select More to display sender account, Bcc box and Priority

9 You can send Bcc (bind carbon copies) and set a priority

10 Right-click to display the App bar with options such as text formatting, hyperlinks and new window

11 To see your email signature, display the Mail Settings, select Accounts and choose the sending account

Note that any changes to the signature text will not affect the current message but will apply to future messages only.

12 Click the Send button to submit the message

A copy of the message is kept in the Sent folder for the sending account.

Should there be any problems with the email addresses used for the recipients, you may receive a message from the Mail Delivery subsystem describing the problem and explaining the reason.

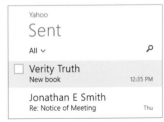

In this case delivery failed because the email address has an unknown domain name and so could not be located.

Calendar

1 Switch to the Start screen and select the Calendar app

150

2 The default is What's next (the events view), but you can easily change this

3 Right-click the screen (or click the narrow bar at the bottom) to display the App bar top and bottom, and select, for example, Month view from the top bar

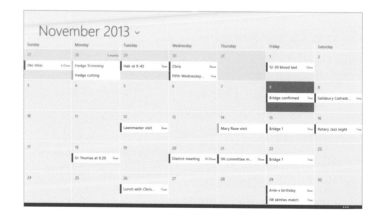

4 Select Week to display seven days at a time (or Work week to display five days, excluding the weekend)

Don't forget

One click of the mouse (or a sideways swipe on a touchscreen) will scroll the calendar one day, one week or one month, depending on the view you have set.

5 Select Day view and you'll normally see two days at the same time. Each day can be separately scrolled

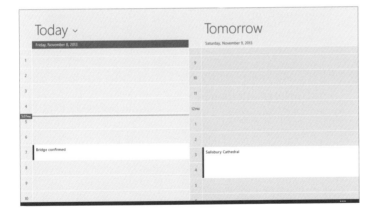

Hot tip

On a higher resolution monitor, 1920 x 1200 for example, the Day view shows three days at the same time.

6 In any view, when you move the mouse, horizontal scroll arrows appear at the top of the screen, one on each side, to help you scroll through your calendar

‹ This week ˅ ›

Skype Instant Messaging

In Windows 8.1, Instant Messaging is supported by the Skype app, rather than the Messaging app that was incorporated with the Mail app in Windows 8.

To set up Skype on your system:

1 Select the Skype tile from the Start screen

2 If desired, allow access to your webcam and microphone

3 You can specify your existing Skype account, or select I'm new to Skype, to use your Microsoft account

152

4 Skype starts up ready for you to add contacts and send instant messages

5 Right-click the Skype screen and select Add contact from the App bar that appears

...cont'd

6 Type a name and press Enter to search your contacts list for Skype details

7 If the details are not found, you are invited to search the Skype directory

You can search the Skype directory to see if you can locate your friends by name or by email address, and then ask to be connected via Skype.

8 Names may give many matches, so it is better to use emails, or actual Skype names if known

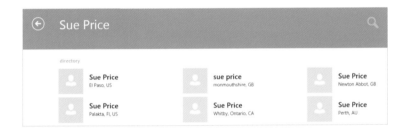

9 When the Skype details are added, send a request to connect via Skype. Your messages and replies are recorded

Your friend must respond to your request before you can engage in online conversations.

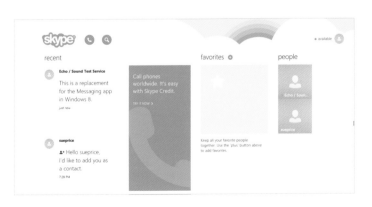

153

Outlook 2013

If you have Windows RT 8.1, or have Microsoft Office 2013 installed on your Windows 8.1 system, you'll have Outlook 2013 as an alternative for email and time management.

Don't forget

The Microsoft Office 2013 tiles and icons may have already been set up on your system, in which case the App bar shows the Unpin options.

1 Display the Apps screen and you'll find the Office applications listed under Microsoft Office 2013

2 Right click and select Pin to Start from the App bar to create tiles on the Start screen

3 Select Pin to Taskbar to add Office icons in the Desktop

4 Select Outlook 2013, from the Apps screen, the Start screen or the Desktop

Welcome to Microsoft Outlook 2013

Welcome to Outlook 2013

Outlook is your personal assistant, helping you manage your life with powerful tools for email, calendar, contacts, and tasks.

Let's get started. In the next few steps, we'll add your email account.

‹ Back   Next ›   Cancel

Hot tip

Unlike the Mail app, Outlook does not automatically detect and connect to your Microsoft account.

5 Click Next and follow the prompts to set up Outlook to connect to an email account. For example, specify your name and the email address and password for your Microsoft account

Outlook is able to configure most types of email account automatically, though you can use manual setup if desired. It will connect to the server, log on and send a test message.

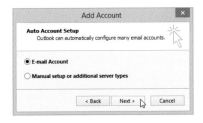

Outlook 2013 is able to configure an email account using a POP server, as in this example.

1 Outlook starts and, if it's the first time you've run an Office application, you are asked to Activate Office

You use the assigned email account to activate Office 365, or the product key for Office 2013. Office RT will already be activated.

2 Use recommended settings to have updates applied, and Outlook is activated

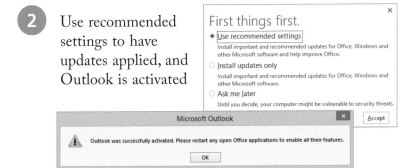

Using Outlook

Click the > to expand the Folder pane (or the < to collapse it). Click the ... on the Navigation menu and clear or select Compact Navigation.

1 Outlook opens in Mail with the most recent message but has buttons for Calendar, People, Tasks etc.

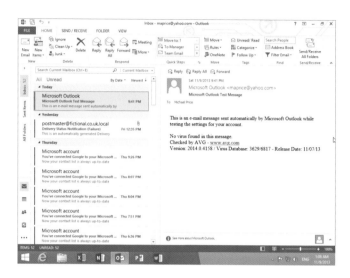

Select View, Reading Pane and choose Off rather than Right or Bottom, to avoid the risks of inadvertently reading spam or phishing emails.

2 Select the View tab and you can display Calendar, People and Tasks alongside the messages

Quick Access Toolbar   Tab bar   Title bar   Help

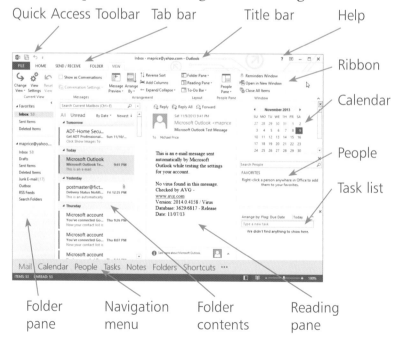

Ribbon

Calendar

People

Task list

Folder   Navigation   Folder   Reading
pane   menu   contents   pane

9 Internet

Windows 8.1 provides two versions of the Internet Explorer browser to help you navigate through the Web, with the full screen Windows app and standard Desktop application. They both offer features such as tabbed browsing, favorites and support for RSS feeds.

Internet Connection

If your computer is connected to your DSL router via an ethernet cable, the connections will usually be set up automatically when you install Windows 8.1, or the first time that you run a new computer with Windows 8.1 pre-installed. No interaction will be required.

If you have a wireless connection to your router, you'll be asked to provide the network key the first time, but connection will be automatic thereafter.

During the installation or first time of use, you may be offered the option to Customize or Use express settings. Select the latter and let Windows set up the network for you.

To review your network settings:

1 On the Desktop, select Settings from the Charms bar and click Control Panel

The connection to your router will be shown as a Private network, suitable for sharing files and printers. If you connect at the office or at an Internet cafe, you'd have a Guest or Public network and should avoid sharing files.

2 From Network and Internet, click View network status and tasks. The Network and Sharing Center opens

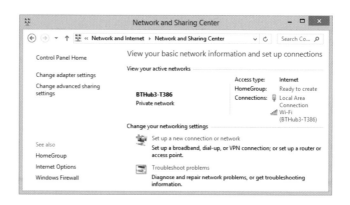

In this example, there are two connections – Local Area Connection (ethernet cable) and Wi-Fi (wireless). Either connection can provide access to the Internet.

3 Click Change adapter settings to see more details of the connections available

...cont'd

To set up an Internet account directly from your computer:

1 In the Network and Sharing Center select the link to Set up a new connection or network

If your network wasn't available at installation time, you can add a connection later.

2 Choose Connect to the Internet to start the

wizard which prompts for the connection type

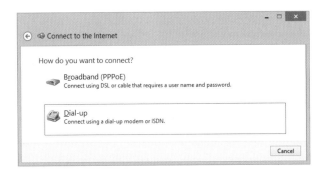

3 Click the type, provide phone number (dialup only), account name, password, etc. and click Connect

If there's already an Internet connection, the wizard will tell you but allow you to continue and define a second connection, for example a dialup backup for your DSL connection.

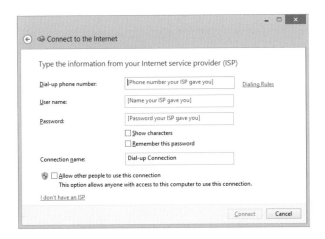

You can allow anyone who has access to this computer to use this connection, or keep it for your own use only.

Browse the Web

Windows 8.1 provides access to the Internet via a browser such as Microsoft's Internet Explorer v11.0. There are two versions – Windows app and Desktop app.

1 Click Internet Explorer on the Start screen to open the Windows app

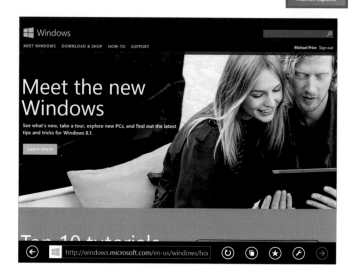

Windows 8.1 does give you the option to specify other browsers such as Mozilla, Opera or Chrome, as the default, but Internet Explorer is used for these examples.

2 The app opens full screen displaying the App bar – this vanishes if you scroll the screen

You can scroll the screen with the mouse wheel, with the scroll bar that appears when you move the mouse, or by dragging on a touch monitor.

...cont'd

3 Right-click an empty part of the Internet Explorer window and the App bar reappears, now combined with Tab switcher

Tabs   New Tab   Tab Tools

Back   Site   Address   Refresh   Tabs   Forward
       Icon   Bar   Page Tools   Favorites

4 Click in the Address bar and begin typing and Internet Explorer will suggest possible web pages

Don't forget

There's no Home page in the Windows app version. It will open the same tabs that you last had open, even after shutting down the system.

161

Don't forget

Internet Explorer keeps a history of the websites that you visit and will make suggestions based on those and upon the Favorites that you may have saved (see page 170). Pinned websites are also searched.

Right-click Menu

The right-click action can vary depending where you click.

 Right-click an empty part (where the mouse pointer remains as an arrow) to get the App bar and Tabs

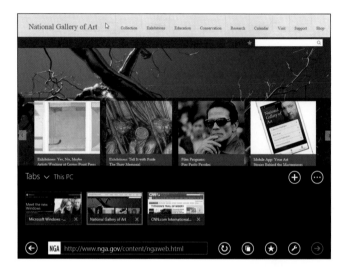

Right-click an image with a hyperlink (where the mouse pointer becomes a hand) and a menu will be displayed

There's a slightly different menu displayed when you right-click text with a hyperlink (again indicated by a hand symbol)

These right-click actions are quite unlike the results that you get with the Desktop Internet Explorer. To explore the differences, view the current web page on the Desktop:

Display the App bar, then click the Page tool and select the option View on the desktop

Pin Websites

Windows app IE can add web pages to Favorites and can also Pin web pages to the Start screen. To add a web page:

The Windows app IE provides the option to rename the Favorite, and to specify the Favorites folder you want to use – All being the top level.

1 Display the web page and the App bar, click the Favorites button, then click Add to Favorites

2 Accept/amend the name and the folder, and click Add

3 Alternatively, select the Pin site button to Start, accept/amend the name, then click Pin to Start

4 From the App bar, click Favorites to see your Pinned web pages, and click All to see your Favorites

The websites that you Pin to Start will, of course, appear on the Start screen as a group of tiles, so you can start Internet Explorer with a Pinned site.

Zoom Web Page

You may find some web pages difficult to read, especially if you have your monitor set for high resolution. The Zoom feature provides an effective solution to this problem.

1 Click the Tools button on the Toolbar and select Zoom

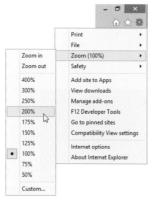

2 Choose a level, e.g. 200%

3 Press Ctrl + to Zoom in, 25% more each time

4 Press Ctrl - to Zoom out, 25% less each time

5 Press Ctrl 0 to return to the 100% level

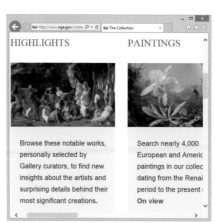

Zoom Button

If you enable the Status bar, you'll find a Zoom button that makes it easier to apply changes to the levels of magnification.

6 Click the Zoom button repeatedly to cycle through the levels 125%, 150% and 100%

...cont'd

The Windows app Internet Explorer will accept the same keyboard shortcuts, but there are no Zoom menus or button.

1 With full screen display always in effect, some web pages may not be easy to view at the default size

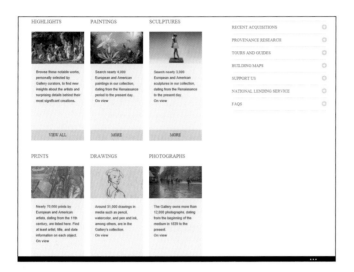

2 Press Ctrl + three times to apply a zoom factor of 175% and the images fill the screen

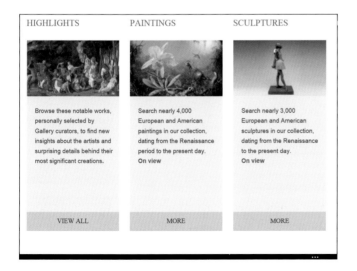

Press Ctrl 0 to return to the 100% zoom level.

If you have a particularly high resolution screen, you can increase the default zoom factor from 100%. From the Internet Explorer app display the Charms bar and select Settings.

Select Options to adjust the Zoom slider where you can set a value between 50% and 400% as the default. This only affects the Windows Internet Explorer app.

RSS Feeds

Internet Explorer tells you whenever there's a feed available, if you enable the Command bar to see the Feeds icon.

1 If there are no feeds available, the button is grayed

2 When you switch to a web page that has a feed, the Feeds button changes color and a sound plays

3 Click the Feeds button and select the feed to view the reports it offers

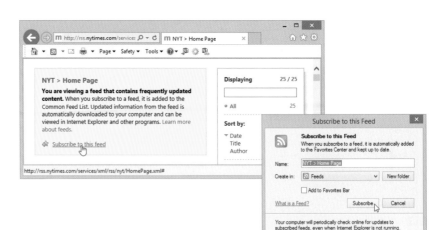

4 If the reports interest you, click Subscribe to this feed, then click Subscribe and you'll be able to view updated content in Internet Explorer or in Windows Live Mail (see page 154)

10 Windows Games

Go to Xbox Games and the Windows Store, to find a variety of products to challenge and teach. You can record your scores and compare your results with other players.

Games in Windows 8.1

In previous releases of Windows, a good selection of games was included in the initial installation. In Windows 7, for example, you'd find the following in the Games folder:

Associated with this folder was the Games Explorer, which helped you to get software updates and news feeds for the installed games. The Games Explorer also tracked wins, losses and other statistics.

You won't find these games in Windows 8.1. In fact, there are no Desktop games actually installed with the system. However, Microsoft is integrating Xbox content and gaming services into Windows. There is a Games app which helps you find Xbox games, available from the Games section of the Windows Store (see page 128), where you'll find many games available.

Xbox

Xbox is a video game console manufactured by Microsoft, first released in 2001. It is a sixth-generation gaming device designed to compete with Sony's PlayStation. The integrated Xbox Live service, launched in 2002, allows players to play games online with a broadband connection.

Games App

1   Click Games on the Start screen and the Games app launches, and signs you in

Welcome to Xbox

We've given you the gamertag SinuousVermin7. Your gamertag is your identity in the online world of Xbox. You can change it once for free at Xbox.com.

Adding an Xbox profile to your Microsoft account opens the door to entertainment in Windows 8. Get the details here.

Your current privacy settings   [**OK**]

The first time you run Xbox, you'll be assigned an accpunt associated with your Microsoft account, and you'll get a gametag to identify you to other players.

2   A selection of Xbox games for the PC is highlighted

3   Select a game, e.g. Minesweeper, to see a description. Click Explore game for more details

4   Click Play to get the game from the Store

The first time you play, you are told that the app needs to be added and you get a link to the Store.

Microsoft® Minesweeper

Microsoft® Studios, Strategy & Simulation
Windows

Top 5 Free Game in the Windows Store! Play the classic puzzle game that has been a part of Windows for more than 20 years, now re-imagined for Windows 8. Featuring adjustable difficulty, classic Minesweeper gameplay, and a brand new Adventure gameplay mode, Microsoft Minesweeper is better than ever. Play Daily Challenges, earn medals, and take your game online with Xbox achievements and leaderboards.

No apps are installed to open this type of link (xboxliveapp-1297290226)

Get "Minesweeper" from the Store

Play
Explore game
Play trailer

Minesweeper

1 Select the link to Get Minesweeper from the Store, to show the description and click the Install button

2 The game is installed and a tile is added to the Start screen

3 Select the tile to start the game

The first time you play, you'll get a gametag assigned to your Microsoft account, to identify you to other players.

4 Choose one of the game types, such as Easy 9x9 to get started, or a more advanced level later

5 The game starts and the first time you play you get hints and prompts to explain how it works

Don't forget

You use the number to help deduce whether a square is safe to uncover. Right-click a suspect square to add a flag, or left-click a safe cell. On a touchscreen, you would press for a flag or tap for a safe cell.

6 If you go wrong the results can be explosive

Hot tip

Your results are stored under your gametag and with the Game app you can view your achievements and share them with your friends.

7 Get it right and you are treated to fireworks

Games at the Windows Store

Don't forget

The games that are highlighted and the numbers of apps shown will change frequently, but these examples illustrate the type of findings you can expect.

1 Open the Windows Store, right-click and select the Games category and Highlighted and Trending apps

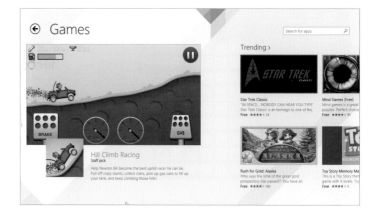

2 Scroll sideways to see the New & Rising, Top paid and Top free games apps, and click Top free

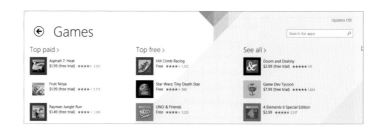

Hot tip

Some of the games shown in the Top free or Top paid sections may also be included in the New & Rising or Highlighted sections.

3 This displays the games in the Top free group, but the number shown is limited to 1,000

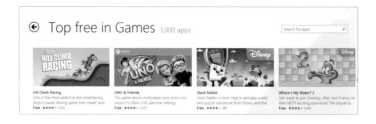

Press the Back arrow to go back to the listing for Games.

...cont'd

4 Click See all to get a full list of Games which is not limited to 1,000 apps (in this example we find 16,578 games)

Don't forget

To check the range of prices, select Sort by highest price, and you'll see prices of $33.99 or lower.

5 Click the down-arrows next to All sub-categories, All prices or Sort by noteworthy, to display the filter options

6 To find out what costs might be involved, choose All sub-categories, Paid and Sort by lowest price

7 Games are sorted by the least expensive first, (4,548 apps shown, starting from $1.49 with a free trial included)

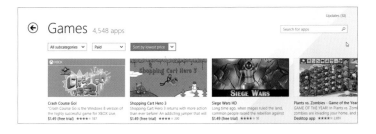

Note that there are many Desktop games apps displayed.

Microsoft Solitaire Collection

1 Find the app in the Store, and click the Install button to download and install the app

Don't forget

If you have enjoyed playing FreeCell or Spider Solitaire in a previous release of Windows, you'll be pleased to find the Microsoft Solitaire Collection in the Store.

2 Pin the app to the Start screen and select the tile

3 The first time, you'll be asked to allow the app to access and update your Xbox Live info

4 The app loads up and offers you a choice of games (Klondike, Spider, FreeCell, Pyramid, TriPeaks) plus a daily challenge

Hot tip

By allowing access, you will have a record of the results for all the games you play and you can share your achievements with other players.

5 Scroll horizontally to review and select a theme

6 Scroll on to the How to play section

7 Select FreeCell for step by step guidance on playing

Microsoft Mahjong

This game has three skill levels, with four puzzles for each, giving 12 in total. It can be played with keyboard, mouse or by touch.

1 Locate the app in the Store, and choose Install to download and install the app, then pin it to the Start screen

2 Select the Tile for the app and the first time you run the app you are asked for permission to access your Xbox Live info

3 Select Choose puzzle

4 You'll start off with just one Easy choice puzzle available to play

As with all the Xbox Live games, you get a record of your scores for all the puzzles and you can compare your results with other players.

5 Each time you that complete a puzzle, the next one will be unlocked and available to play

6 Click matching pairs of free tiles to remove them

Right-click the play area and you'll see an App bar with buttons giving access to How to play, Pause, Hint and New game.

7 If you get stuck, press H for a hint and two matching tiles will flash

8 Fireworks are displayed when you complete the game and the next puzzle gets unlocked

Congratulations

'TriPeak' now unlocked!

OK

If there's a particular puzzle you like to relax with, select it and Pin it to the Start screen to make it easy to get.

9 Press the back arrow to go back to the main screen

10 Scroll horizontally and you'll find Themes, Awards, Statistics, Leaderboards and finally How to play, with tutorial, controls and tips and tricks

Microsoft Mahjong

How to play

🔍 Play Tutorial

🎴 Overview

👆 Controls

⌨ Keyboard controls

❓ Tips and tricks

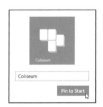

Word Games

Don't forget

Not all games are as complex as Mahjong and Solitaire. There are simple games that are easy and fun to play, for example Word Games.

1 Go to the Store and use the Search for apps box to look for the term "word search". Our search found 480 apps

2 Select the entry for Wordsearch to install it and pin it to Start

3 Click Wordsearch on the Start screen

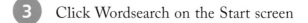

4 Select a game mode, the difficulty level and a category and click Start

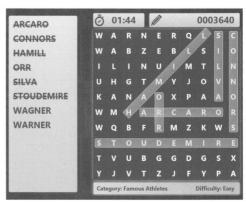

5 Locate the words in the panel

6 Even with a simple game, you can use the mouse, keyboard or touch to select the letters that make the words

7 When you finish, you are offered the option to specify a player name and to submit your scores online

Hot tip

You don't have to worry about providing a name and recording your scores, unless you do like keeping track of your results.

11 Music and Pictures

With the sound card in your system, you can create recordings, play audio CDs and convert tracks to computer files to build and manage a music and sound library. You can also store and manage digital pictures and videos and create movies from your photos and video clips.

Sound Card and Speakers

The sound card in your computer processes the information from programs such as the Music app or Windows Media Player and sends audio signals to your computer's speakers.

Hot tip

The sound card on your system may be incorporated into the system board, or may be provided as a separate adapter card.

To review and adjust your sound setup:

1 Press WinKey + X to open the Power Users menu and select Control Panel

2 Select Hardware and Sound and then Sound

3 Click the Playback tab, select the entry for speakers and click Configure

4 Select your speaker setup and click Test to check the speakers and then click Next to continue

Don't forget

Click Test to hear a sound from each speaker, or click an individual speaker to hear a sound from it, to ensure all speakers are working.

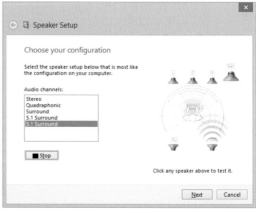

...cont'd

5 Specify which speakers are present in your setup

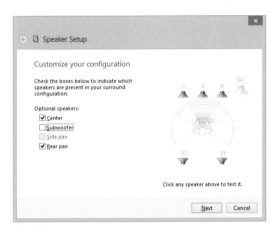

6 Specify if speakers are full range versus satellite

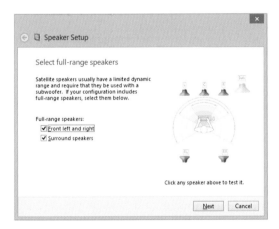

7 Click Finish to complete and apply the configuration

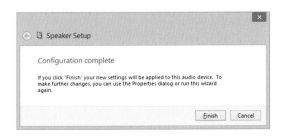

If you have a laptop or tablet PC with built in speakers these will normally be stereo and full-range.

If you have a separate sound adapter, it may be installed with its own audio application programs to set up, configure and test the device features.

Recording

With a sound card on your system, you can make voice recordings from a microphone or other audio sources. To set up your microphone:

1 Open the Sound option from the Control Panel and click the Recording tab

2 Select the Microphone entry and click Configure

3 Select Set up microphone and select the type you are using (headset, desktop or other kind)

4 You should set up your microphone according to the recommendations, to ensure clear and effective recordings

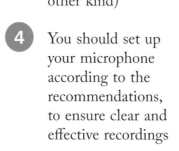

...cont'd

5 Read the sample text and follow the prompts to set up the microphone for the best recording

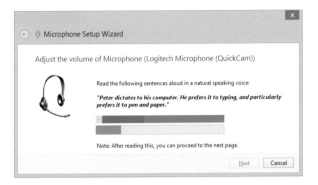

If there are problems with the level of recording, you may be asked to go back and try again, perhaps avoiding background noise.

6 Your microphone is now set up. Click Finish

Repeat the microphone configuration and take the Speech Tutorial, or train your computer to better understand your voice.

With the microphone set up, you can now use a program such as Audio Recorder from the Windows Store, to record and play audio notes. These can be stored on your SkyDrive, so you can share them and access them from any computer.

191

Play Audio CD

Hot tip

You also use your sound adapter and speakers to play music from a CD or files that you download from the Internet.

Don't forget

If you accept the recommendations, Windows Media Player becomes the default for music files. Information about the music is downloaded and usage data will be sent to Microsoft.

1 Insert an audio CD and close the drive

2 Windows recognizes the type of disc and prompts you (if a default action isn't yet defined)

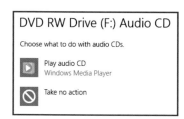

DVD RW Drive (F:) Audio CD
Tap to choose what happens with audio CDs.

3 You can choose to Play audio CD (using Windows Media Player) or Take no action, whenever audio CDs are inserted

> DVD RW Drive (F:) Audio CD
>
> Choose what to do with audio CDs.
>
> ▶ Play audio CD
>   Windows Media Player
>
> ⊘ Take no action

4 Click Play audio CD. Windows Media Player starts and the first time you must choose the settings

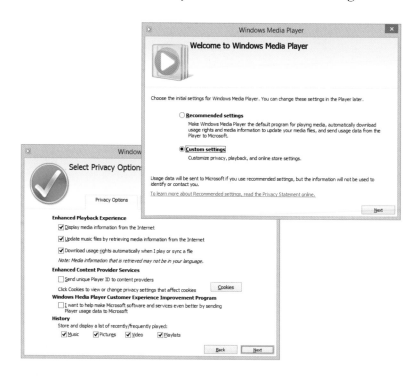

5 Click Custom settings to review and if necessary make changes to the Privacy options that are applied

...cont'd

 **6** Make Windows Media Player the default, or choose the file types that you want it to handle

 **7** The CD begins to play and track data is added

 **8** Move the mouse over the window and click the Switch to Library button that appears, to see details

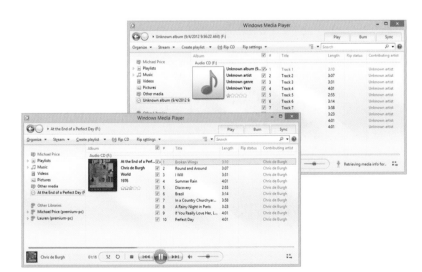

 Don't forget

Windows Media Player is the only option offered for playing CDs. However, to play music files there is a Music app (see page 196) you can use.

Don't forget

The CD just provides the track numbers and the durations, but the CD is identified and the full artist and album details are downloaded.

 193

Copy Tracks

1 Right-click Now Playing, select More Options, then click the Rip Music tab

2 For Format, choose the type of audio file (e.g. MP3)

3 Choose the Audio Quality (e.g. using bit rate 192 Kbps)

4 Start playing the CD and click the Rip CD button (it becomes Stop rip and then CD Already Ripped)

5 Each track in turn is copied, converted and saved

6 Files will be saved by default in your Music folder

Beware

The higher the bit rate, the better the quality but the larger the file. As an estimate, a full audio disc copied at:

Bit rate	Needs
128 Kbps	57 MB
192 Kbps	86 MB
256 Kbps	115 MB
320 Kpbs	144 MB

Don't forget

You can play the CD while tracks are being independently copied (at a multiple of the standard play speed – the whole CD may be completed before the first track finishes playing).

Media Library

The converted tracks will be saved in the specified location, (the Music folder), in an album under the artist's name.

Don't forget

Type Windows media on the Start screen and press Enter. If you plan to use this often, you can Pin it to the Taskbar or the Start screen (see page 69).

To explore the albums stored on your hard disk and to play tracks from them:

1 Start the Windows Media Player and click the Library button to switch to the Library view

2 Choose how to display the contents of the Music library, e.g. by Album or by Artist

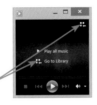

Hot tip

To include folders in Windows Media Player, you add them to the appropriate Windows folder, either Music, Pictures, Recorded TV or Videos.

3 Double-click an artist to display their albums, then double-click one of the albums to start it playing

Music App

1 Select Music from the Start screen to launch this full screen Windows app

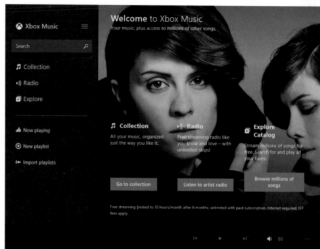

Hot tip

If you want to play music on a tablet or netbook PC, you might prefer the simplicity of the Music app. As usual, you sign in to this app using your Microsoft account.

2 You are signed in to Xbox Music, and you see a menu with Search, Collection, Radio and Explore

Don't forget

When you sign in to the Music app for the first time, it finds all the music files stored in your Music folder and makes them available as your Collection.

All done! We've added the music from this PC.

3 Select Collection to see all the music on your system, arranged by album and by date added

...cont'd

4 Click Radio to set up your own radio stations based on the artists you prefer plus similar music

Click Start a station and specify an artist name, and Xbox Music will set up a play list. You can define as many as you wish. Click Now playing for details of the particular tracks being played.

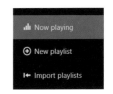

5 Select Explore to browse the contents of the Xbox Music catalog, starting with the New albums listed

You may see and hear adverts as you explore the Catalog. You can purchase an Xbox Music Pass to eliminate ads (see page 198).

6 Click Show all to see more albums, and select the genre, e.g. Pop, Rock, Dance, Soundtrack or Classical

197

Xbox Music Features

Hot tip

Click the down arrow next to the Results heading to see what matches there are for In Collection and Full Catalog.

1 You can enter a descriptive term and Search in your Collection or the Catalog (for Radio or Explore)

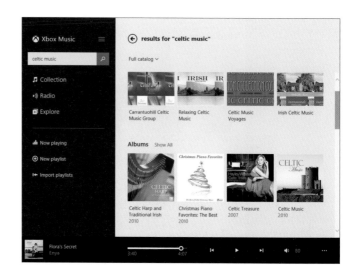

You have free streaming access to the music you find in the Catalog for the first six months. However, after this period, it is limited to 10 hours per month.

2 Click Learn more to get details of the ad-free subscription service, the Xbox Music Pass

Hot tip

The Music app takes advantage of Windows Snap to display the web page on the same screen. However, you can display the page full screen, as shown in Step 3.

3 You are offered a 30 day free trial, after which the subscription is $9.99 per month (*at the time of printing*)

With Xbox Music Pass you have unlimited ad-free streaming, and offline listening on PC, tablet or phone, with the devices kept automatically in sync.

Alternatively, you can share music in your Collection with other computers.

4 Display the Charms bar for the Music app, click Settings and select Preferences then Find out how this works

The music in your collection is matched against the Xbox Music catalog, and those that are found are made available, at no charge, on your other devices.

Digital Pictures

There are a number of ways you can obtain digital pictures:

- Internet (e.g. art and photography websites)
- Scanner (copies of documents, photographs or slides)
- Digital Camera (photographs and movies)
- Email attachments and faxes

Website pictures will usually be stored as JPEG (.jpg) files, which are compressed to minimize the file size. This preserves the full color range but there is some loss of quality. Some images such as graphic symbols and buttons will use the GIF (.gif) format, which restricts color to 256 shades to minimize the file size. To copy a digital image from a website such as **www.nga.gov**:

Don't forget

The Desktop Internet Explorer is used for these examples, but you can do similar actions with the Internet Explorer Windows app, though you do get different menus (see page 162).

Hot tip

You can right-click and save the picture even when only part of it is visible on the screen.

Hot tip

Click Browse Folders to select a folder and create a subfolder, e.g. using artist name, to organize the saved images.

① Right-click the image and select Save picture as...

② Type a suitable file name and click Save

3 Select Start, Pictures and select the appropriate subfolder to list and view the saved images

Hot tip

Windows 8.1 includes a number of picture viewers you can use to examine your downloaded pictures (see page 202).

Websites may sometimes offer you the option to download higher quality images. For example, **www.wikipaintings.org/en/john-constable/flatford_mill-1817**:

1 This entry shows Constable's Flatford Mill (Scene on a Navigable River) at a size of 500 x 409 pixels

2 Scroll down and click Show sizes, and you'll see there are images ranging from a 65 x 65 thumbnail to a full resolution image 2024 x 1656 pixels

Beware

Images downloaded from websites are usually copyrighted and provided for personal use only.

Viewing Pictures

Hot tip

To make more space in the folder, click the Navigation pane button and turn off that pane.

Don't forget

You can change the Photo Viewer default by selecting Settings from the Charms bar, then Change PC Setting, Search and apps, and Defaults.

1 Open the Pictures folder in File Explorer, select View and choose Extra large icons and Preview pane

2 You can explore the folder and view specific pictures

3 To view a picture more closely, double-click to open in the default app, usually the Photos app

4 To choose a different app, right-click the file icon, select Open with and choose an app

5 To change the default, right-click the file, select Open with and then click Choose default program and select one from the list

Photos App

1 The Photos app opens, showing the selected picture

Click the + in the corner to zoom. Click the scroll buttons to view other photos in the same folder.

2 Right-click to display the Apps bar for photos

On the Apps bar, there are seven action buttons for individual photos, including Edit. For Folders there are just four buttons.

3 Click the back arrow to show the containing folder and select Thumbnail view or Details view

Click the down arrow next to the folder name to switch between the Pictures library and your SkyDrive.

203

...cont'd

Don't forget

From the Photos app, display the Charms bar, select Settings and then Options, and you can turn on or off the live display of photos on the Photos tile.

← Options

Shuffle photos on the Photos tile

On

4 Display the Apps bar for a photo and click the Edit button to see the fixes and effects supported

5 Click the Zoom button to inspect changes closely

Beware

If you select Cancel, you'll be asked to confirm before the changes are discarded.

You're about to lose any changes you've made.

Cancel anyway

6 Right-click to display the App bar and Undo changes, Save a copy, Update original or Cancel changes

Windows Photo Viewer

The supplied alternative to Photos app is Windows Photo Viewer, a Desktop application.

1 Select a picture and choose Open with Windows Photo Viewer

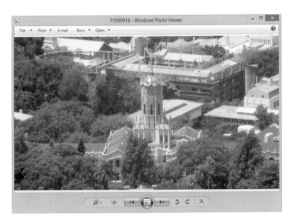

Don't forget

You can select Picture Tools in the Library folder and click the Slide show button to start Windows Photo Viewer and display your pictures.

2 Controls include Magnify, Actual size, Previous, Play slide show, Next, Rotate left, Rotate right and Delete

3 Click Play slide show to run a full screen slide show with the pictures

4 Right-click the window to display the menu and change the settings or Exit the slide show

Hot tip

You can change the size of file that is sent, or specify Original size.

5 From the Menu bar, you can Print, Email or Burn picture files to CD or DVD

Note that when you email pictures they will, by default, be attached as reduced size files.

```
Smaller: 640 x 480
Small: 800 x 600
Medium: 1024 x 768
Large: 1280 x 1024
Original Size
```

Photo Gallery, Movie Maker

If you install the Windows Essentials 2012, free applications provided by Microsoft, you will have two additional options for handling photos and videos

For more information or to download the applications, visit the website **http:// windows.microsoft. com/en-us/windows-live/essentials**

1 Photo Gallery provides powerful facilities to import, edit, view and share photos, pictures and video clips

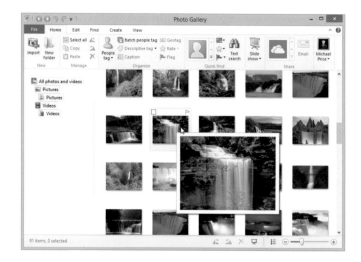

Move the mouse over a picture icon and a preview image immediately appears.

2 Movie Maker helps you make more advanced movies from your videos and photographs, and publish them to YouTube, Facebook and other Internet locations

The AutoMovie feature allows you to quickly turn your slides into a movie with music or audio incorporated.

12 Networking

Create a home network, wired or wireless, to share drives, printers and Internet access. Windows 8.1 computers can create or join a HomeGroup, to share media libraries with other computers and devices on the network.

Create a Network

Hot tip

Unlike devices that are attached directly to a computer, the devices on a network operate independently of one another.

You have a network when you have several devices that exchange information over a wire or over radio waves (wireless). The simplest network consists of one computer and a router that links to the Internet. You can add a second computer, to share Internet access and exchange information with the other computer. If the PCs are Windows 8/8.1- or Windows 7-based, a HomeGroup can help with sharing data.

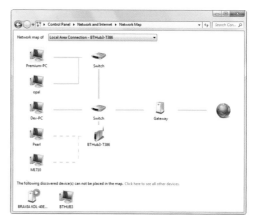

Hot tip

This network map is from the Windows 7 PC. There's no map in Windows 8.1, but it does show network computers and devices (see page 214).

To make the connections, your network will require:

1. Ethernet twisted-pair cables, for the wired portion

2. A router to manage the network connections

3. An Internet modem, which may be integrated with the router

4. An adapter for each computer (wired or wireless)

To implement your network, you'll need to carry out actions such as these:

Don't forget

Windows 8.1 detects the presence of a network and will automatically set up the computer to participate and to create or join a HomeGroup (for a home networks only).

● Install the necessary network adapters
● Establish the Internet Connection
● Set up the wireless router
● Connect the computers and start Windows

Network Classification

1. Install the network adapter (if required) and start up Windows (with no network connection)

2. Display the Charms bar and select Settings. The Network icon shows Unavailable

3. Add a cable between the adapter and the router and the Network shows as named and connected

Windows will detect the network and give it a default classification, but you can override its choice.

4. Click the Network icon, right-click the Network and click Turn sharing on or off

5. Choose No, for networks in public places

This gives a **Public network** for networks in places like coffee shops or airports, or for guests to access. HomeGroup is not available and network discovery is turned off.

6. Choose Yes for networks at home or at work

This gives a **Private network** for home or work networks or for known and trusted environments. The computer can join a HomeGroup and Network discovery is turned on.

Often, there will be a network adapter built into your computer. If not, you'll need to install an adapter card or add a USB adapter.

The classification is shown in the Network and Sharing Center (see page 216).

BTHub3-T386
Public network:

BTHub3-T386
Private network

Network discovery allows you to see other computers and devices on the network and allows other network users to see your computer. Turning Network discovery off hides your computer.

Create HomeGroup

If you set up a Private network and no HomeGroup has yet been established, you are given the option to create one.

Don't forget

If a HomeGroup has already been created on the network, you get the option to join that HomeGroup (see page 213).

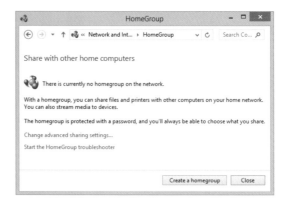

Beware

If the other computers on your network are powered off or hibernating, a new computer might think there is no HomeGroup. In that case, just click Close.

1 To confirm you want to share with other home computers, click Create a homegroup

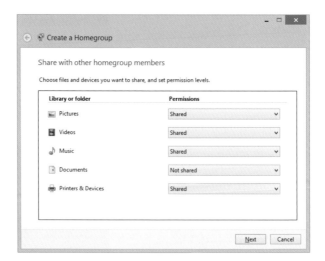

2 Specify what types of data or devices you want to share then click Next

By default, you'll share your Pictures, Music, Videos and Printers, but not your Documents. However, you can change any of these to Shared or Not shared, as desired.

...cont'd

Windows will automatically generate a secure password for the HomeGroup for you to share with other network users.

Don't forget

Windows uses a random combination of lower case, upper case and numbers. However, you can change the password to something more easily remembered, if you wish.

3 Make a note of the new password and click Finish

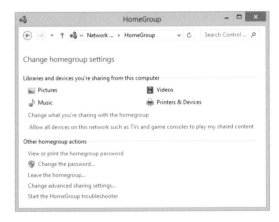

Hot tip

Note the option to allow all devices on the network, including TVs and games consoles, to access your shared content.

4 View the HomeGroup settings and make any changes if required. You can also view or print the password, or change it to a more memorable password

5 Click Close for the HomeGroup Settings and do remember to share the password with the other users

Connect to Wireless Network

Cabled PCs usually get added automatically. When you bring a new wireless PC into the network, you'll need to set up the connection.

Beware

Your system may detect other wireless networks that are in the vicinity, so make sure to select the correct entry.

212

Don't forget

Your computer will now always connect to that network when it comes into range. You can have numerous wireless connections defined, for example home, office and Internet cafe.

1 Display the Charms bar, select Settings, note the Network icon indicates Available networks

2 Click the icon to display the connections and choose your main wireless network

3 Click in the box to Connect automatically and then click Connect

4 Enter the network security key for your wireless network and click Next

5 If this is the first time the computer has been connected to the network, you'll be asked to specify the network classification – Private or Public

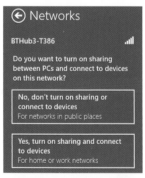

6 Your computer will now show as connected to the wireless network

Join the HomeGroup

1 Windows tells you about the existing HomeGroup. Click Join now, or click Close if you are not joining

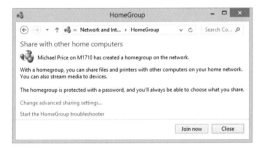

When you add a new cabled or wireless PC to a Private network, you may be invited to join the HomeGroup.

2 Choose the items you want to share and click Next

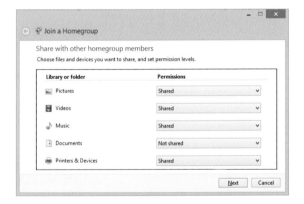

Windows may take a few minutes to set up sharing, so you should not shut down the computer until you are told that you have joined the HomeGroup.

3 Type the HomeGroup password and click Next

4 Click Finish when prompted and you have joined

View Network Devices

There's no Network map facility in Windows 8.1, unlike Windows 7 (see page 208). However, you can find a list of all the computers and other devices that are connected and active on your network.

Don't forget

You can also display the Charms bar, select Search and then select Settings, to carry out a Settings search.

1 Press WinKey + W to display Search Settings, type View network devices and select the entry for View network computers and devices

2 The File Explorer program opens on the Desktop with the Network category selected

Don't forget

Alternatively, go to the Desktop, open File Explorer from the Taskbar icon and select the Network category.

3 This shows all the computers, network devices such as hubs, media devices such as Internet-connected TVs and shared media libraries

Hot tip

Only devices that are currently active will show up.

4 Click the HomeGroup category to view its members

View HomeGroup

1 Open File Explorer and select HomeGroup to display the users on the network who are members

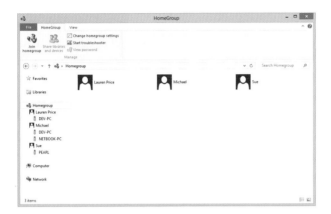

Hot tip

If a computer on the network is powered off or hibernates, its entries are removed. When a computer is powered up, its entries are added. To ensure the display is up to date, right-click and select Refresh.

2 Expand the entries to see the computer names. You may have a user signed on at two or computers, or have more than one active user on one computer

3 Double-click a user's entry to see what libraries and devices are available for sharing

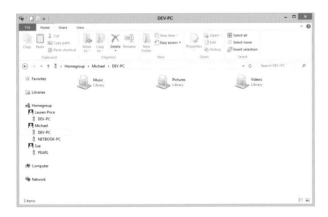

Hot tip

If you choose not to create the HomeGroup initially, you'll see the Ready to create option in the Network and Sharing Center.

4 Double-click a library entry to explore its contents. You can access other users' libraries as if they were your own

Network and Sharing Center

1 Display Search Settings, type Network center and select the entry for Network and sharing center

Alternatively, open the Control Panel and click View network status and tasks.

You can also right-click the Network icon on the Taskbar and select Open Network and Sharing Center.

2 View the basic information for your active networks

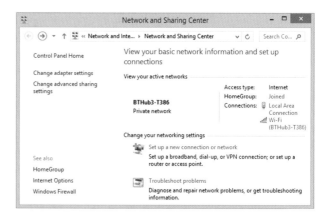

3 Click Change advanced sharing settings, to review the options for Private and for Public networks

You'll see that Private networks usually have Network discovery and File and printer sharing turned on. For Public networks, these are usually turned off.

1 Click HomeGroup in the Network and Sharing Center, to view and change HomeGroup settings

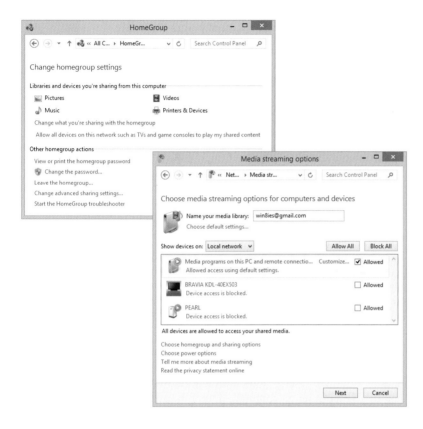

Hot tip

This panel is displayed when you create or join the HomeGroup. This link from the Network and Sharing Center allows you to revise your initial settings.

2 Click the link Allow all devices on this network, to choose media streaming options and click Allow All, then click Allow all computers and media devices

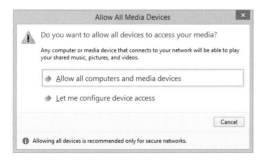

Beware

As noted, the option to allow all devices is recommended only for secure networks.

PC Settings

Don't forget

You can also open Search Settings and look for entries related to HomeGroup.

1 Open the Charms bar, select Settings and then click Change PC settings

2 Select the Network entry and then the HomeGroup entry

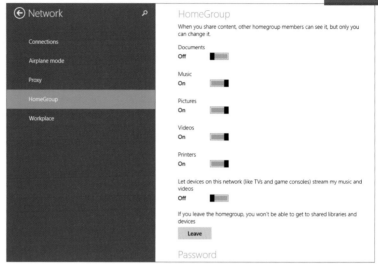

3 You can easily turn access on or off for the individual devices and libraries. There is a Leave HomeGroup button, and the Password for joining is stored there

4 Select Connections for Wi-Fi and Network status

Hot tip

The individual wireless devices that you might find on your computer could include Wi-Fi, Mobile broadband and Bluetooth. Airplane mode switches all of them on or off with one click.

5 Select Airplane mode to turn off all your wireless devices when you are traveling

13 Security & Maintenance

Help and support is enhanced by online access to the latest information and there are other ways of getting useful advice. Windows Action Center keeps track of your system and a variety of system tools help protect your computer from hazards.

Windows Help

Most functions in Windows are supported by wizards, which make the tasks easier by providing prompts and suggestions. However, there is a comprehensive help system when you do need answers to questions.

Hot tip

You can also press F1 while at the Desktop, to open Windows Help and Support.

1 From the Start screen, type Help and press Enter

2 Windows Help and Support displays on the Desktop

220

3 You may see a message at the top of the screen saying you are not connected to the Internet

Don't forget

If the online Help service is unavailable, it remains in Offline mode, but you will still get local help and support information.

4 Check your Internet connection

5 Restart Help and Support, or click the Offline Help button and select Get online Help, to be sure you get the most up-to-date help

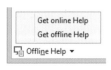

6 Click Get Started to see what's new in Windows 8.1

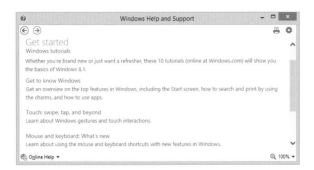

If the particular topic you want doesn't appear when you scroll the Help pages, type a suitable search phrase in the Search box and click the Find button.

7 Click Get to know Windows, to view new features

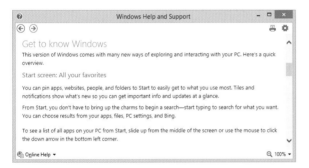

8 Click the back arrow and select Touch: Swipe, tap and beyond, to learn about Windows 8.1 gestures

In keeping with its Online status, the Help and Support information can be expected to change over time, so the contents you see on your system may differ.

More Support Options

If you can't find the answer you are seeking in the Help information, you can ask Support or other users for help.

1 In Windows Help and Support, click Contact support

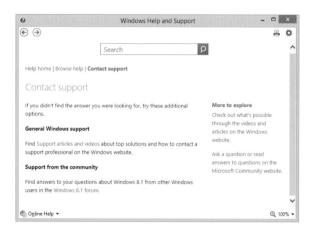

The forum contains answers to questions about Windows 8.1, from the Microsoft support team and from other Windows users.

2 Click the link for the Windows 8.1 forum and review questions and answers, or submit your own

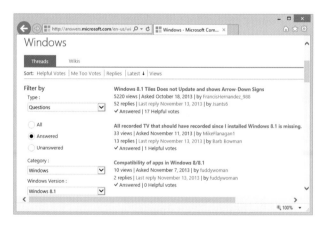

Show all Windows topics, or select a specific topic that you want to explore in more detail.

3 From Windows Help and Support, click the link to explore the Windows website for articles and videos

4 Search your computer manufacturer's website for Windows 8.1-related updates and information

Product Solution Centers

Microsoft offers solution centers for many products, Windows 8.1 included. To view the list of solution centers:

1 Open **http://support.microsoft.com** and select the area of interest, or click More products for a full list

The solution centers, categories and topics listed will change from time to time, so you could revisit the website periodically.

2 Select a topic that interests you, for example Xbox

3 At the Xbox site, choose subtopic, e.g. Games and Windows 8

4 You'll be shown specific information related to your interest, in this case PC Games

Right-click a topic and select Open in new tab or Open in new window, to keep the solution center available.

5 Explore to find items such as patches for games or manuals for games, or hints and tips about how to get the most out of the applications

Windows Action Center

The security and maintenance features in Windows 8.1 are monitored in the Windows Action Center. You will be alerted by an icon message in the notification area.

Hot tip

You can also select Action Center by right-clicking the icon.

Alternatively, Search Settings on the Start screen and select Action Center.

224

1 Click the icon to see the message summaries, then click Open Action Center

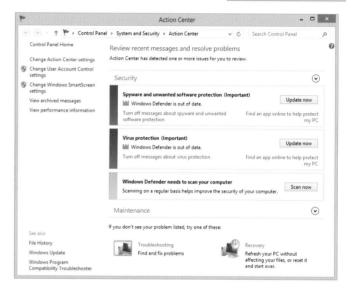

Don't forget

Red shows important items that should be dealt with quickly, such as antivirus software. Yellow items are suggested tasks such as maintenance activities.

2 Action Center warns you when your spyware or virus protection needs installing or updating

3 You may be reminded to run a scan using Windows Defender, the software included in Windows

4 You will be reminded if there are problems you have not yet reported to Microsoft

5 Action Center also has links to Troubleshooters and to Recovery tools

Program Compatibility

Windows 8.1 helps you deal with older programs.

1 Right-click the Alerts icon and select Troubleshoot a problem, then select Run programs made for previous versions of Windows

2 Click Next to find and fix problems with running older programs in Windows 8.1

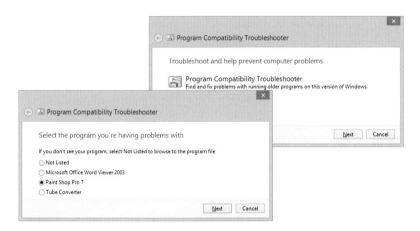

3 Select the program and Try recommended settings

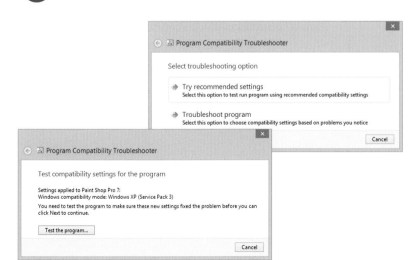

Alternatively, you can search Settings for Compatibility, to locate and run the Compatibility troubleshooter.

You must test run the program to see if the selected settings work before you can continue and complete the troubleshooter.

Windows Firewall

1 Open Control Panel, select System and Security and click Windows Firewall

Don't forget

To protect your computer from malicious software while it is connected to the Internet, you need Firewall software. This is included as part of Windows.

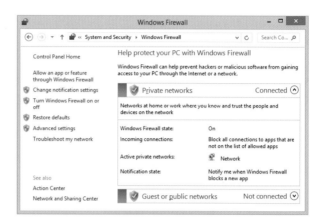

2 Click Allow a program or feature through Windows Firewall, to view the list of allowed programs

Don't forget

Programs may be added automatically when applications are installed, for example the Mail and Messenger apps.

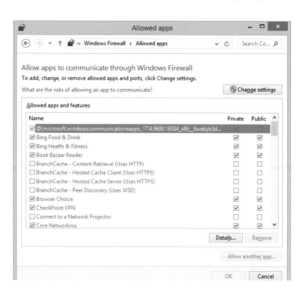

3 Click Change settings to change or remove allowed features and apps and to enable Allow another app

Windows Defender

1 On the Start screen, type Defend and select the Windows Defender program

2 Windows Defender opens to display the latest status

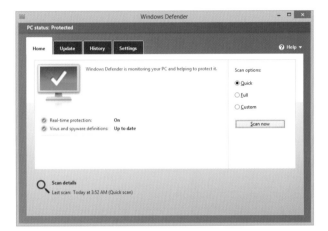

3 Click Scan now and Windows Defender will carry out a quick scan of your computer and report results

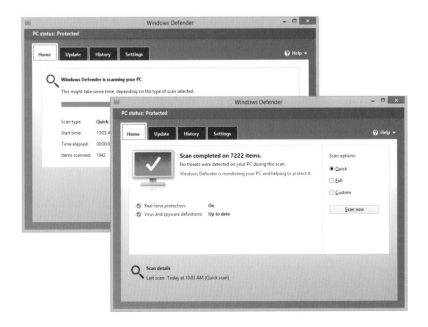

Windows Defender provides protection against malicious software such as viruses and spyware, so you do not have to install separate utilities.

The Action Center may also alert you and offer to run a scan.

Windows Defender also alerts you when spyware attempts to install or run, or when programs try to change important Windows settings.

Windows Update

To review the process by which software updates are added to Windows:

1 Right-click the Alerts icon and select Open Windows Update, or select Control Panel, System and Security, Windows Update

Updates are changes or additions that will help fix or prevent problems, enhance operation or improve performance.

2 Windows displays the status and gives a summary of the settings that are currently in effect

If Windows Update is not switched on, you'll see an alert in the Notification area and a message in the Action Center.

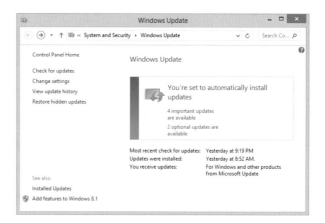

3 Select the Change settings command to see the full list of settings, ready for any changes

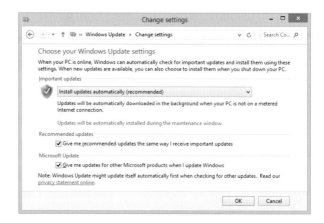

4 Click the Important updates box and the list of options is displayed (with Automatic recommended)

Don't forget

If you have an always-on broadband connection, you should allow Windows to apply updates automatically.

5 Click the link Install updates automatically and you will see the Automatic Maintenance window

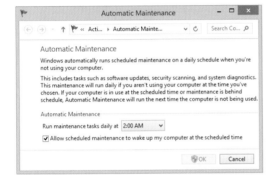

Hot tip

Updates are installed automatically at 3:00 AM unless you specify a different time. If the PC is not active at that time, updates are installed the next time you shut down.

6 For the full screen Windows Update status, display the Charms bar, select Settings and Change PC Settings and click Windows Update

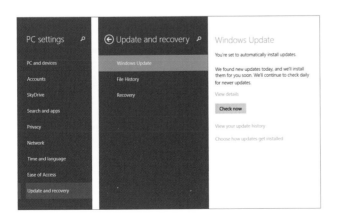

Beware

The full screen Windows Update is for status display only and does not offer any facilities for changing settings, etc.

System Restore

Problems may arise when you install new software or a new device. If uninstalling does not correct the situation, you can return the system files to their values prior to the changes.

Restore points are created every day and just before any significant change such as an installation or update. You can also open System Protection and create a restore point yourself.

Select a date and time that's prior to the problems and then click Next to restore the settings to that point in time.

1 Open Control Panel, then System and Security and then click System

2 Select the System Protection entry

3 Click the System Restore button

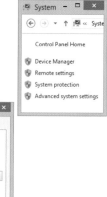

4 System Restore recommends the restore before the most recent change, but you can choose another one

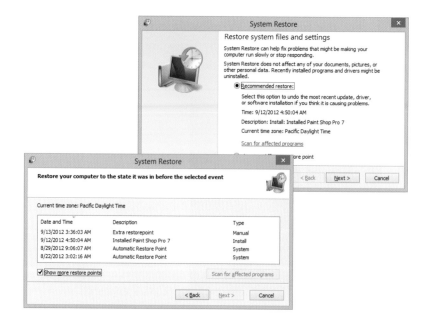

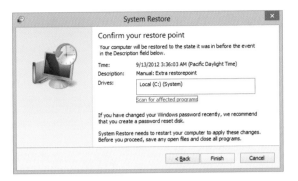

5 Click Finish to confirm your selected restore point

Once started, System Restore cannot be interrupted, though it can be undone (unless run from Safe Mode or the System Recovery Options menu).

6 On restart, System Restore confirms restore

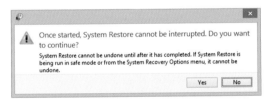

7 You can still run System Restore to undo the restore

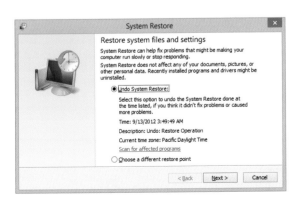

If the selected restore point does not resolve your problems, you can undo the restore and try a different restore point.

File History

Don't forget

You can lose files accidentally, as a result of a virus, or due to software or hardware failure. To protect your data, you must keep copies of your files.

Hot tip

Backup copies are created every hour by default, but you can change the frequency. Backups are kept forever, but you can specify a time limit.

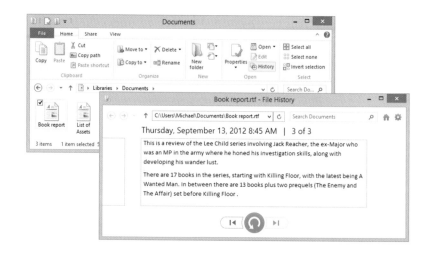

Don't forget

To browse through the backups, select File History and click Restore personal files.

1 Open Control Panel, then System and Security and then click File History

File History
Save backup copies of your files with File History
Restore your files with File History

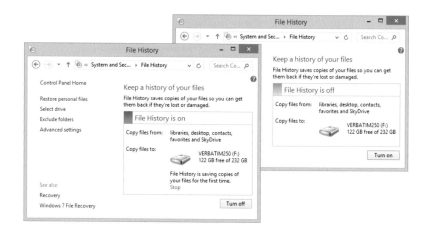

2 File History identifies an external or network drive to use for backup and you then select Turn on

3 An initial backup of your files is taken and regular backups of changes are carried out thereafter

4 Select a file in File Explorer and click the History button to see all its backups in a Player style display

Index

M

236

N

O

X

Y

Z